AF727075

Comprehensive Insights into Artificial Intelligence Techniques for Transformer Condition Assessment

Dr. M. KARTHIK

Ms. A. DEEPIKA

Ms. G. HEMALATHA

Copyright © <2024> <Dr. M. KARTHIK>

All Rights Reserved.

This book has been self-published with all reasonable efforts taken to make the material error-free by the author. No part of this book shall be used, reproduced in any manner whatsoever without written permission from the author, except in the case of brief quotations embodied in critical articles and reviews.

The Author of this book is solely responsible and liable for its content including but not limited to the views, representations, descriptions, statements, information, opinions and references. The Content of this book shall not constitute or be construed or deemed to reflect the opinion or expression of the Publisher or Editor. Neither the Publisher nor Editor endorse or approve the Content of this book or guarantee the reliability, accuracy or completeness of the Content published herein and do not make any representations or warranties of any kind, express or implied, including but not limited to the implied warranties of merchantability, fitness for a particular purpose. The Publisher and Editor shall not be liable whatsoever for any errors, omissions, whether such errors or omissions result from negligence, accident, or any other cause or claims for loss or damages of any kind, including without limitation, indirect or consequential loss or damage arising out of use, inability to use, or about the reliability, accuracy or sufficiency of the information contained in this book.

Made with ❤ on the Notion Press Platform

www.notionpress.com

Contents

Preface

In the rapidly evolving world of electrical power systems, the role of transformers is both critical and complex. These essential components are responsible for adjusting voltage levels and ensuring the efficient distribution of electricity across vast networks. Given their importance, maintaining their health and operational efficiency is paramount. Traditional methods of monitoring and maintenance, while valuable, are increasingly being complemented—and sometimes replaced—by advanced technologies. Among these, Artificial Intelligence (AI) stands out as a game-changer.

"Comprehensive Insights into Artificial Intelligence Techniques for Transformer Condition Assessment" is born out of a growing need to understand and harness AI's transformative potential in the field of transformer maintenance. This book is intended to bridge the gap between theoretical knowledge and practical application, offering a thorough exploration of AI techniques tailored for evaluating transformer health.

Our journey begins with an introduction to the challenges faced in transformer monitoring and the limitations of conventional approaches. From there, we delve into the core of AI methodologies, breaking down complex concepts into accessible insights. The book covers a range of topics, including machine learning, deep learning, and predictive maintenance strategies, and how they can be applied to enhance transformer condition assessment.

Each chapter is designed to provide a clear understanding of AI techniques and their real-world applications. We explore machine learning algorithms that predict health metrics and detect faults, and examine deep learning methods that analyze intricate data patterns. Practical case studies are interwoven throughout the text to illustrate successful implementations and offer readers a glimpse into the practical benefits of AI in transformer maintenance.

As the field of AI continues to evolve, so too does the potential for its application in transformer health assessment. This book aims to provide readers with not only the knowledge of current technologies but also an understanding of future trends and innovations. By equipping professionals, researchers, and engineers with a comprehensive view of AI's capabilities, we hope to foster advancements in transformer maintenance that lead to more reliable and efficient power systems.

We would like to extend our gratitude to the many colleagues and industry experts who contributed their insights and experiences, making this book possible. Your dedication to advancing knowledge and technology in this field is truly inspiring.

Thank you for embarking on this journey. We hope that **"Comprehensive Insights into Artificial Intelligence Techniques for Transformer Condition Assessment"** serves as a valuable resource and a source of inspiration for those committed to pushing the boundaries of what is possible in transformer health monitoring.

22.08.2024

Dr. M. KARTHIK

Ms. A. DEEPIKA

Ms. G. HEMALATHA

Acknowledgments

The journey of bringing **"Comprehensive Insights into Artificial Intelligence Techniques for Transformer Condition Assessment"** to fruition has been both challenging and rewarding, and it would not have been possible without the support and contributions of many individuals and organizations.

First and foremost, I wish to acknowledge the grace and guidance of God, whose blessings have made this endeavor possible. Without divine inspiration and strength, this book would not have come to fruition. I am deeply grateful for the wisdom and support provided through this journey.

I would like to extend my deepest thankfulness to Sri Ramakrishna Engineering College, Coimbatore and SRM Madurai College for Engineering and Technology, Pottapalayam for providing the academic environment and resources that have been crucial to the development of this book. The support and encouragement from the faculty and administration have been instrumental in the completion of this work.

I extend my heartfelt gratitude to Notion Press for their belief in this project and for their exceptional support throughout the publishing process. Your commitment to advancing technical literature has been instrumental in bringing this book to life.

A sincere thanks to my colleagues (**Ms. A. DEEPIKA , Ms. G. HEMALATHA**) and mentors in the fields of electrical engineering and artificial intelligence. Your invaluable insights, feedback, and encouragement have profoundly shaped the content of this book.

I am also deeply appreciative of the industry professionals and researchers who generously shared their real-world experiences and case studies. Your contributions have added a practical dimension to the book that enhances its relevance and value.

To my family and friends, I offer my deepest thanks for your patience, understanding, and unwavering support during the writing process. Your encouragement has been a source of strength and inspiration.

Finally, I extend my gratitude to the broader community of readers, engineers, and researchers dedicated to advancing transformer health assessment. Your pursuit of knowledge and innovation drives the progress in our field and inspires works like this.

Thank you all for your support and contributions. It has been an honor to work with you, and I hope this book serves as a valuable resource for all who engage with it.

Dr. M. KARTHIK

1. Introduction to Transformer Health Assessment

Transformers are pivotal elements in electrical power systems, designed to transfer electrical energy between circuits through electromagnetic induction and play a crucial role in stepping up or stepping down voltage levels for efficient power transmission and distribution. Their primary function is to adjust voltage levels to minimize energy loss during long-distance power transmission, making them indispensable in ensuring that electricity reaches consumers reliably and efficiently. Given their critical role, maintaining the health of transformers is of paramount importance to prevent failures that can lead to widespread power outages, equipment damage, and substantial financial losses. Effective transformer health assessment involves a comprehensive evaluation of several key factors. Insulation condition is one of the most critical aspects; it includes both solid insulation, such as paper and pressboard, and liquid insulation, typically transformer oil, which must be monitored to prevent degradation that can lead to failures. Electrical parameters, including voltage, current, and power factor, are crucial for assessing the operational efficiency of the transformer and detecting anomalies. Thermal conditions also play a significant role, as transformers generate heat during operation, and overheating can indicate excessive load or cooling issues, potentially accelerating insulation degradation. Mechanical integrity, which encompasses the physical condition of the core, windings, and connections, is essential for ensuring proper operation. Environmental conditions such as ambient temperature, humidity, and pollution can also impact transformer health and should be carefully monitored.

To assess transformer health, both offline and online methods are employed. Offline testing, which requires taking the transformer out of service, includes techniques such as insulation resistance testing, which measures the resistance of the insulation system, and power factor testing, which assesses the quality of the insulation. These tests provide detailed insights into the condition of the transformer but necessitate downtime. Online methods, on the other hand, allow for continuous monitoring without disrupting service. Techniques such as dissolved gas analysis (DGA) measure the concentration of gases dissolved in transformer oil, which can indicate potential issues like overheating or arcing. Temperature monitoring is another online method, providing real-time data on the operational temperature of the transformer to detect overheating issues. Regular health assessments through these methods are crucial for extending the lifespan of transformers, ensuring their reliability, and preventing costly downtimes. Properly conducted assessments allow utilities to identify and address potential issues proactively, ensuring that transformers continue to operate efficiently and reliably, thereby supporting the stability and efficiency of the entire power grid.

1.1 Overview of Transformer Components and Their Functions

Transformers are essential devices in electrical power systems, designed to adjust voltage levels through electromagnetic induction. Their operation relies on a variety of components, each with a specific function that contributes to the overall efficiency, safety, and performance of the transformer. Understanding these components and their roles is crucial for comprehending how transformers work and for ensuring their proper maintenance and operation.

Core

The **core** of a transformer is one of its most critical components. Made from laminated sheets of silicon steel, the core provides a low reluctance path for the magnetic flux generated by the current flowing through the windings. The core is typically constructed from thin, insulated steel laminations to reduce energy losses due to eddy currents and hysteresis. By efficiently channeling the magnetic flux between the primary and secondary windings, the core facilitates effective electromagnetic induction, which is fundamental to the transformer's ability to transfer electrical energy from one circuit to another. The core's design, including its shape (such as rectangular, cylindrical, or toroidal) and material properties, directly impacts the transformer's efficiency and performance.

Windings

The **windings** are another crucial component of a transformer. They consist of coils made from conductive materials, such as copper or aluminum, and are typically wrapped around the core. There are two main types of windings in a transformer:

- **Primary Winding**: This winding is connected to the input power source and carries the incoming voltage. When alternating current (AC) flows through the primary winding, it generates a magnetic field around the core.
- **Secondary Winding**: The secondary winding is connected to the output load and receives the voltage transferred through the magnetic field from the primary winding. The voltage level in the secondary winding is determined by the turns ratio between the primary and secondary windings.

The number of turns in each winding determines the transformer's voltage ratio. For example, if the secondary winding has more turns than the primary winding, the transformer steps up the voltage; if it has fewer turns, the transformer steps down the voltage. The design and quality of the windings are critical for efficient energy transfer and minimal energy loss.

Insulation System

The **insulation system** is vital for ensuring the safe and reliable operation of a transformer. It consists of both solid and liquid insulation materials:

- **Solid Insulation**: This includes materials such as paper, pressboard, and plastic. Solid insulation provides electrical isolation between the windings and between the windings and the core, preventing short circuits and electrical breakdown.
- **Liquid Insulation**: Transformer oil is the most common type of liquid insulation. It serves multiple functions, including electrical insulation, cooling, and protection against moisture. The oil's insulating properties help to maintain high dielectric strength, preventing electrical failures.

The insulation system's effectiveness is crucial for the transformer's longevity and operational safety. Over time, insulation can degrade due to factors like thermal stress, electrical stress, and chemical reactions, necessitating regular inspection and maintenance.

Cooling System

Transformers generate heat during operation due to electrical losses and core losses. Therefore, an effective **cooling system** is essential to dissipate this heat and maintain the transformer's temperature within safe operating limits. Cooling systems can be broadly categorized into:

- **Air Cooling**: This is often used in smaller transformers and involves the use of natural or forced air circulation to cool the transformer. Fans or blowers may be employed to enhance air circulation and improve cooling efficiency.
- **Oil Cooling**: In larger transformers, oil cooling is commonly used. Transformer oil circulates through the core and windings, absorbing heat and transferring it to radiators or cooling fins, where it is dissipated into the atmosphere. This method is effective for maintaining optimal operating temperatures.

- **Oil-to-Water Cooling**: Some transformers use a combination of oil and water cooling. The oil absorbs heat from the transformer, which is then transferred to a water-cooled heat exchanger or radiator system. This method provides enhanced cooling performance and is used in high-capacity transformers.

Proper cooling is essential to prevent overheating, which can lead to accelerated insulation degradation, reduced efficiency, and potential transformer failure.

Bushings

Bushings are insulating devices that allow electrical conductors to pass through the transformer's outer casing while maintaining electrical insulation and protection from environmental elements. They are typically mounted on the transformer tank and provide connections for both the primary and secondary windings. Bushings consist of an insulating material, such as porcelain or composite, and are designed to withstand electrical stresses and environmental conditions. Proper functioning of bushings is critical for maintaining electrical safety and preventing electrical faults.

Tap Changer

A **tap changer** is an important component that adjusts the voltage ratio between the primary and secondary windings to regulate the output voltage according to load conditions. Tap changers can be classified into:

- **Off-Load Tap Changers**: These require the transformer to be de-energized for adjustments. They are typically used for infrequent voltage adjustments and are manually operated.
- **On-Load Tap Changers**: These allow for voltage adjustments while the transformer is in operation. They are equipped with mechanisms that enable automatic or manual voltage regulation under load conditions, which helps to maintain stable output voltage despite variations in load.

Tap changers are essential for voltage regulation and maintaining power quality in the electrical grid.

Protection Devices

Protection devices are crucial for safeguarding transformers and connected equipment from electrical faults and abnormal conditions. Key protection devices include:

- **Circuit Breakers**: These devices automatically disconnect the transformer from the power source in the event of a fault, such as a short circuit or overload, to prevent damage and ensure safety.
- **Fuses**: Fuses provide overcurrent protection by melting and interrupting the circuit when the current exceeds a predefined limit. They are typically used in conjunction with other protection devices to provide reliable fault protection.
- **Relays**: Protective relays monitor electrical parameters such as current, voltage, and temperature, and activate circuit breakers or alarms in response to abnormal conditions.
- **Current Transformers (CTs)** and **Voltage Transformers (VTs)**: These instrument transformers provide scaled-down replicas of current and voltage for measurement and monitoring purposes, allowing for accurate assessment of electrical parameters and enabling effective protection and control.

Enclosure or Tank

The **enclosure** or **tank** houses all the internal components of the transformer, including the core, windings, insulation system, and cooling equipment. It provides structural support and protects the internal components from environmental factors such as moisture, dust, and physical damage. The tank is typically made of steel and is often filled with transformer oil to provide additional insulation and cooling. The design of the tank includes features such as inspection covers, cooling fins, and access points for maintenance and monitoring.

Monitoring and Instrumentation

Modern transformers are equipped with various **monitoring and instrumentation** systems that provide real-time data on their operating conditions. These systems include:

- **Temperature Sensors**: These sensors measure the temperature of the transformer oil and windings, providing critical information for managing cooling and preventing overheating.
- **Dissolved Gas Analysis (DGA)**: This technique measures the concentration of gases dissolved in transformer oil, which can indicate the presence of electrical faults, overheating, or insulation degradation.
- **Partial Discharge Monitors**: Partial discharge monitoring detects localized electrical discharges within the insulation system, which can signal insulation weaknesses and potential failure.

- **Condition Monitoring Systems**: These systems integrate various sensors and data analysis tools to continuously assess the transformer's health, performance, and operational status.

Effective monitoring is essential for early fault detection, preventive maintenance, and ensuring the overall reliability of the transformer.

In summary, transformers are complex devices with multiple components, each serving a specific function to ensure efficient and reliable operation. The core and windings facilitate electromagnetic induction and voltage transformation, while the insulation system provides electrical isolation and cooling. Cooling systems, bushings, and tap changers contribute to maintaining optimal operating conditions and voltage regulation. Protection devices safeguard the transformer and connected equipment from faults, and the enclosure or tank protects the internal components from environmental factors. Monitoring and instrumentation systems provide real-time data for assessing transformer health and performance. Understanding these components and their functions is crucial for effective transformer maintenance and operation, ultimately supporting the stability and efficiency of the electrical power grid.

1.2 Importance of Transformer Health Monitoring

Transformers are essential components of the electrical grid, performing the critical function of voltage transformation to ensure efficient power transmission and distribution. Given their importance, monitoring the health of transformers is paramount for maintaining the reliability, efficiency, and safety of the electrical power system. Transformer health monitoring involves a range of practices designed to assess the condition of transformers, detect potential issues early, and prevent failures. This essay explores the importance of transformer health monitoring by examining its benefits, methodologies, and impact on the power system.

Preventing Transformer Failures

One of the primary reasons for transformer health monitoring is to prevent unexpected failures. Transformers are subject to various stressors, including electrical, thermal, and mechanical loads, which can lead to degradation over time. Key issues such as insulation breakdown, overheating, and mechanical damage can cause transformer failures. These failures can lead to severe consequences, including power outages, equipment damage, and financial losses. By continuously monitoring transformer health, utilities can identify potential issues before they escalate into catastrophic failures.

Early detection of problems allows for timely maintenance or replacement, reducing the risk of unplanned outages and ensuring a more reliable power supply.

Enhancing Reliability and Stability

Transformer health monitoring plays a crucial role in enhancing the reliability and stability of the electrical power system. Transformers are vital for maintaining voltage levels and ensuring efficient power distribution. A failure in a transformer can disrupt the entire power grid, leading to widespread outages and instability. By employing health monitoring practices, utilities can ensure that transformers operate within their optimal parameters and identify potential risks that could affect system stability. Regular monitoring helps in managing the load on transformers and adjusting operations to prevent overloading, thereby maintaining the stability and reliability of the power system.

Extending Transformer Lifespan

Transformers are significant investments, and their replacement or repair can be costly. Health monitoring is essential for extending the lifespan of transformers by enabling proactive maintenance and addressing issues before they cause significant damage. Monitoring techniques, such as insulation resistance testing, dissolved gas analysis (DGA), and thermal imaging, provide valuable insights into the condition of key components. By addressing wear and tear early, utilities can prolong the operational life of transformers, maximizing the return on investment and delaying the need for costly replacements.

Optimizing Maintenance Practices

Effective maintenance is critical for ensuring the longevity and reliability of transformers. Health monitoring provides valuable data that helps in optimizing maintenance practices. Traditional maintenance schedules may not align with the actual condition of the transformer, leading to either premature maintenance or inadequate intervention. Health monitoring allows for condition-based maintenance, where maintenance activities are performed based on the actual condition of the equipment rather than a fixed schedule. This approach ensures that maintenance resources are allocated efficiently, reducing costs and minimizing the impact on transformer operation.

Reducing Operational Costs

Proactive health monitoring can significantly reduce operational costs by preventing major failures and optimizing maintenance. Unexpected transformer failures can lead to costly repairs, emergency response actions, and replacement costs. Additionally, prolonged outages can result in financial losses due to disrupted power supply and damage to connected equipment. By implementing health monitoring practices, utilities can reduce the likelihood of such costly events. Regular monitoring helps in identifying minor issues that can be addressed before they escalate, leading to lower maintenance and repair costs and improved operational efficiency.

Improving Safety

Transformer failures can pose significant safety risks, including electrical fires, explosions, and hazardous material releases. Insulation breakdown or overheating can lead to dangerous conditions that jeopardize the safety of personnel and the surrounding environment. Health monitoring helps in identifying potential safety hazards by detecting issues such as insulation degradation, overheating, and gas accumulation. Early detection of these issues allows for timely intervention, reducing the risk of accidents and ensuring a safer working environment for maintenance personnel and the public.

Enhancing Environmental Protection

Transformers use insulating oils that, if leaked or spilled, can have harmful environmental effects. Monitoring the condition of the transformer and its insulating oil helps in preventing leaks and minimizing environmental impact. Techniques such as dissolved gas analysis (DGA) can detect the presence of gases that may indicate insulation degradation or potential leaks. By monitoring these factors, utilities can take preventive measures to avoid environmental contamination and comply with regulatory requirements for environmental protection.

Supporting Grid Modernization and Smart Grids

The ongoing modernization of power grids and the implementation of smart grid technologies emphasize the need for advanced transformer health monitoring. Smart grids rely on real-time data and advanced analytics to enhance grid performance, reliability, and efficiency. Transformer health monitoring is integral to this evolution, providing the data needed for advanced grid management and optimization. By integrating health monitoring data with smart grid technologies, utilities can enhance grid resilience, improve load management, and support more efficient power distribution.

Compliance with Standards and Regulations

Utilities and power companies must adhere to various industry standards and regulations concerning transformer operation and maintenance. Health monitoring helps ensure compliance with these standards by providing the necessary documentation and data to demonstrate that transformers are being maintained and operated according to regulatory requirements. Compliance with standards not only avoids potential fines and penalties but also promotes best practices in transformer management and operation.

Real-world examples highlight the importance of transformer health monitoring. For instance, a major power outage caused by transformer failure in a large city can result in significant economic losses and disrupt essential services. By implementing robust health monitoring practices, utilities in these regions can detect early signs of transformer issues and take preventive measures to avoid such failures. Case studies of successful transformer monitoring programs demonstrate how timely interventions and condition-based maintenance can lead to improved reliability, reduced costs, and enhanced overall system performance.

In summary, transformer health monitoring is of critical importance for maintaining the reliability, efficiency, and safety of the electrical power system. By preventing failures, enhancing reliability, extending transformer lifespan, optimizing maintenance practices, and reducing operational costs, health monitoring ensures the smooth operation of transformers and the stability of the power grid. It also contributes to safety, environmental protection, and compliance with industry standards. As the power industry continues to evolve with advancements in smart grid technologies, transformer health monitoring will remain a vital component in supporting grid modernization and enhancing overall system performance.

1.3 Challenges in Traditional Transformer Health Assessment Methods

Transformers are crucial components in the electrical power grid, and their reliability is vital for the stability and efficiency of power distribution. Traditional methods of assessing transformer health have been the backbone of maintenance practices for decades, but these methods face several challenges that can affect their effectiveness and efficiency. This essay explores the challenges associated with traditional transformer health assessment methods, including their limitations, practical difficulties, and the impact on transformer reliability and performance.

Limitations of Offline Testing

Traditional transformer health assessment methods primarily rely on offline testing, which involves taking the transformer out of service to conduct diagnostic tests. While offline testing provides detailed insights into the condition of the transformer, it presents several limitations:

- **Service Interruption**: Offline testing requires the transformer to be de-energized, leading to service interruptions. This can affect the reliability of the power supply and cause disruptions, especially in critical applications or during peak demand periods. The need to take the transformer offline for testing can lead to operational inefficiencies and inconvenience.
- **Inconvenience and Cost**: The process of de-energizing a transformer, performing tests, and then re-energizing it can be time-consuming and costly. This includes not only the direct costs of testing but also the indirect costs associated with service interruptions and potential impacts on the power grid. Additionally, the logistics of scheduling and coordinating offline testing can be complex and resource-intensive.
- **Limited Frequency of Testing**: Due to the inconvenience and cost associated with offline testing, it is typically performed at infrequent intervals. This limited testing frequency can result in delayed detection of emerging issues, reducing the ability to proactively manage transformer health and potentially leading to unanticipated failures.
- **Data Interpretation**: The data obtained from offline tests can be challenging to interpret accurately. Diagnostic tests often provide snapshots of the transformer's condition at a specific point in time, which may not fully represent the dynamic nature of transformer operation and potential issues that develop over time.

Challenges in Insulation Testing

Insulation testing is a critical component of traditional transformer health assessment, as insulation condition directly impacts transformer performance and reliability. However, insulation testing faces several challenges:

- **Aging Insulation**: Over time, insulation materials such as paper and pressboard can degrade due to thermal stress, electrical stress, and environmental factors. Traditional insulation testing methods may not fully capture the complex degradation processes occurring within the insulation system, leading to incomplete or inaccurate assessments.

- **Limited Diagnostic Capability**: Insulation testing methods, such as insulation resistance measurements, primarily assess the overall condition of the insulation system but may not detect localized faults or subtle degradation. For example, insulation resistance testing may not identify partial discharge activities or insulation weaknesses that can lead to failure.
- **Complexity of Insulation Systems**: Modern transformers often have complex insulation systems that include multiple layers and materials. Traditional testing methods may struggle to provide a comprehensive assessment of these intricate systems, leading to potential gaps in understanding the true condition of the insulation.

Issues with Dissolved Gas Analysis (DGA)

Dissolved Gas Analysis (DGA) is a widely used technique for monitoring the condition of transformer oil and detecting potential faults such as overheating or arcing. Despite its importance, DGA presents several challenges:

- **Interpretation of Gas Levels**: DGA involves measuring the concentration of gases dissolved in transformer oil, such as hydrogen, methane, ethane, and acetylene. While elevated levels of specific gases can indicate fault conditions, interpreting these gas levels can be complex. The relationship between gas concentrations and specific fault types may not always be straightforward, leading to potential misinterpretation of the results.
- **Sensitivity to Oil Quality**: The accuracy of DGA results can be affected by the quality and condition of the transformer oil. Contaminants, oxidation, and other factors can impact gas solubility and affect the reliability of the analysis. In cases where the oil quality is compromised, DGA may not provide an accurate representation of the transformer's condition.
- **Frequency of Testing**: Like other offline testing methods, DGA requires periodic sampling and analysis, which may not align with the dynamic nature of transformer operation. Infrequent testing can lead to delays in detecting emerging issues and may not capture transient or intermittent faults.

Challenges in Thermal Imaging

Thermal imaging is used to detect hot spots and temperature anomalies in transformers, which can indicate potential issues such as overheating or faulty connections. Despite its benefits, thermal imaging has its own set of challenges:

- **Limited Resolution**: Thermal imaging cameras may have limitations in resolution and sensitivity, which can affect their ability to detect small or subtle temperature variations. In transformers with complex configurations or densely packed components, thermal imaging may not provide sufficient detail for accurate diagnosis.
- **Temperature Gradients**: Transformers often experience temperature gradients across different components and operational conditions. Thermal imaging may struggle to differentiate between normal temperature variations and abnormal hot spots, potentially leading to false positives or missed issues.
- **Environmental Factors**: External factors such as ambient temperature, sunlight, and weather conditions can impact the accuracy of thermal imaging. Ensuring consistent and reliable measurements requires careful consideration of these environmental factors, which can complicate the assessment process.

Practical Difficulties in Mechanical Inspections

Mechanical inspections of transformers involve examining physical components such as the core, windings, bushings, and tap changers. While visual and physical inspections can provide valuable insights, they face several challenges:

- **Accessibility**: Some transformer components may be difficult to access, particularly in large or enclosed installations. Mechanical inspections may require specialized equipment or disassembly, which can be time-consuming and disruptive.
- **Subjectivity**: Visual inspections are often subjective and rely on the experience and expertise of the inspector. Assessing the condition of components based on visual observations alone may lead to inconsistent or inaccurate evaluations.
- **Detection of Hidden Issues**: Mechanical inspections may not always detect hidden or internal issues, such as internal insulation faults or core damage. Some problems may only become apparent during operation or through more advanced diagnostic techniques.

Integration and Data Management Issues

Traditional assessment methods often involve multiple data sources and testing techniques, which can create challenges in data integration and management:

- **Data Fragmentation**: Traditional methods may generate data from various sources, such as insulation resistance tests, DGA, and thermal imaging. Integrating and correlating this data to obtain a comprehensive understanding of the transformer's condition can be complex and may require manual effort.
- **Lack of Real-Time Data**: Many traditional methods provide data at discrete intervals rather than continuously. This lack of real-time monitoring can limit the ability to detect and respond to issues as they arise, potentially leading to delayed maintenance or corrective actions.
- **Data Interpretation and Analysis**: Analyzing and interpreting data from multiple traditional assessment methods can be challenging. Ensuring accurate diagnosis and decision-making requires expertise and experience, and there may be a risk of overlooking important indicators or trends.

Cost and Resource Implications

Traditional assessment methods can have significant cost and resource implications:

- **High Costs**: The costs associated with offline testing, specialized equipment, and laboratory analysis can be substantial. These costs may include not only the direct expenses of testing but also the indirect costs associated with service interruptions and potential impacts on the power grid.
- **Resource Intensiveness**: Traditional methods often require specialized personnel, equipment, and facilities. Coordinating and executing these assessments can be resource-intensive and may strain maintenance budgets and personnel.
- **Limited Coverage**: Due to the cost and complexity of traditional methods, they may be applied selectively or at infrequent intervals. This limited coverage can result in gaps in monitoring and an incomplete understanding of transformer health.

Impact on Transformer Reliability and Performance

The challenges associated with traditional assessment methods can impact the overall reliability and performance of transformers:

- **Delayed Detection of Issues**: Infrequent testing and limited coverage can lead to delayed detection of emerging issues, increasing the risk of unexpected failures and service interruptions.
- **Inadequate Diagnosis**: Limitations in testing methods may result in inadequate diagnosis of transformer problems, leading to incomplete or incorrect maintenance actions.
- **Increased Risk of Failure**: The inability to detect and address issues proactively can increase the risk of transformer failure, impacting power reliability and leading to potential financial and operational consequences.

Traditional transformer health assessment methods, while foundational to maintenance practices, face several challenges that can impact their effectiveness and efficiency. These challenges include limitations in offline testing, issues with insulation and dissolved gas analysis, difficulties in thermal imaging and mechanical inspections, data management and integration problems, and cost and resource implications. Addressing these challenges requires a combination of improved assessment techniques, advanced diagnostic tools, and enhanced data integration practices. As the power industry evolves, incorporating more advanced and real-time monitoring methods can help overcome the limitations of traditional approaches and ensure more effective management of transformer health.

2. Fundamentals of Artificial Intelligence

Artificial Intelligence (AI) is a multidisciplinary field that aims to create machines capable of performing tasks that would typically require human intelligence. From early conceptualization to contemporary applications, AI has evolved dramatically, impacting various sectors such as healthcare, finance, and transportation. Understanding the fundamentals of AI involves exploring its core concepts, types, methodologies, and the implications of its applications. This essay delves into the foundational aspects of AI, providing a comprehensive overview of its key components and their significance.

Defining Artificial Intelligence

Artificial Intelligence can be broadly defined as the simulation of human intelligence processes by machines, especially computer systems. These processes include learning (the acquisition of information and rules for using it), reasoning (using rules to reach approximate or definite conclusions), and self-correction. The ultimate goal of AI is to develop systems that can operate autonomously and adapt to changing circumstances with minimal human intervention.

AI encompasses various subfields and methodologies, but its core objective remains the creation of intelligent agents—machines that can perceive their environment, make decisions, and take actions to achieve specific goals. The scope of AI extends from basic tasks such as data classification to complex activities like natural language understanding and autonomous driving.

Types of Artificial Intelligence

AI is typically categorized into three types based on its capabilities and functions:

- **Narrow AI (Weak AI)**: This type of AI is designed to perform a specific task or a narrow range of tasks. It operates within a limited domain and lacks generalization abilities. Examples include virtual assistants like Siri and Alexa, recommendation systems used by streaming services, and image recognition software. Narrow AI systems excel at their designated tasks but cannot perform beyond their programmed capabilities.
- **General AI (Strong AI)**: General AI refers to a type of AI that possesses the ability to understand, learn, and apply intelligence across a broad range of tasks at a human-like level. It

can generalize knowledge and adapt to new situations without requiring specific programming for each task. General AI remains largely theoretical and has not yet been realized in practice.

- **Artificial Superintelligence (ASI)**: Artificial Superintelligence represents a level of AI that surpasses human intelligence across all domains, including creativity, problem-solving, and social interactions. ASI is a hypothetical concept and poses both profound opportunities and significant risks. The development of ASI raises ethical and existential questions about the future of humanity and the control of advanced AI systems.

Core Components of AI

The core components of AI involve several key areas that collectively contribute to the development and functionality of intelligent systems:

- **Machine Learning (ML)**: Machine Learning is a subset of AI that focuses on the development of algorithms that allow computers to learn from and make predictions based on data. ML models improve their performance over time as they are exposed to more data. Common ML techniques include supervised learning (where models are trained on labeled data), unsupervised learning (where models identify patterns in unlabeled data), and reinforcement learning (where models learn through trial and error).
- **Natural Language Processing (NLP)**: NLP is a branch of AI that deals with the interaction between computers and human language. It enables machines to understand, interpret, and generate human language. NLP applications include language translation, sentiment analysis, chatbots, and voice recognition systems. NLP combines linguistics and machine learning techniques to process and analyze large volumes of text and speech data.
- **Computer Vision**: Computer Vision involves the development of algorithms that enable machines to interpret and understand visual information from the world. It allows computers to recognize objects, faces, and scenes in images and videos. Applications of computer vision include facial recognition systems, autonomous vehicles, and medical imaging analysis. Computer vision techniques often involve deep learning models, particularly convolutional neural networks (CNNs).
- **Robotics**: Robotics is a field that integrates AI with physical machines to perform tasks autonomously or semi-autonomously. Robotics involves designing and building robots that can interact with the physical world and execute tasks ranging from manufacturing to healthcare. AI

techniques are employed to enhance robotic capabilities, including perception, decision-making, and control.

- **Expert Systems**: Expert Systems are AI applications designed to mimic the decision-making abilities of human experts in specific domains. These systems use a knowledge base of facts and rules to provide solutions or recommendations for complex problems. Expert systems are used in fields such as medical diagnosis, financial analysis, and troubleshooting technical issues.

Machine Learning Techniques

Machine Learning is a crucial subset of AI that involves the use of algorithms and statistical models to enable computers to learn from data. Key ML techniques include:

- **Supervised Learning**: In supervised learning, models are trained on labeled datasets, where each input is paired with a corresponding output. The model learns to map inputs to outputs based on this training data and can then make predictions on new, unseen data. Common algorithms used in supervised learning include linear regression, decision trees, and support vector machines.
- **Unsupervised Learning**: Unsupervised learning involves training models on unlabeled data to identify patterns or groupings without predefined outcomes. Techniques such as clustering (e.g., k-means clustering) and dimensionality reduction (e.g., principal component analysis) are used to uncover hidden structures in the data. Unsupervised learning is useful for exploratory data analysis and anomaly detection.
- **Reinforcement Learning**: Reinforcement learning is based on the principle of learning through interaction with an environment. An agent takes actions to maximize cumulative rewards over time, receiving feedback in the form of rewards or penalties. Reinforcement learning algorithms, such as Q-learning and deep Q-networks (DQN), are used in applications like game playing, robotics, and autonomous driving.
- **Deep Learning**: Deep Learning is a subset of ML that employs neural networks with multiple layers (deep neural networks) to model complex patterns in data. Deep learning has achieved significant breakthroughs in areas such as image and speech recognition, natural language processing, and generative modeling. Techniques include convolutional neural networks (CNNs) for image processing and recurrent neural networks (RNNs) for sequential data.

Ethical and Social Implications

The development and deployment of AI technologies raise several ethical and social considerations:

- **Bias and Fairness**: AI systems can perpetuate or amplify biases present in training data, leading to unfair or discriminatory outcomes. Ensuring fairness and mitigating bias in AI systems require careful design, diverse data representation, and ongoing evaluation.
- **Privacy**: AI applications that involve data collection and analysis can pose privacy concerns, particularly when dealing with sensitive personal information. Data protection and privacy regulations, such as the General Data Protection Regulation (GDPR), play a critical role in safeguarding individuals' rights.
- **Job Displacement**: The automation of tasks through AI and robotics can lead to job displacement and changes in the labor market. Addressing the impact on employment requires strategies for workforce retraining and adaptation to new roles created by technological advancements.
- **Accountability and Transparency**: The decision-making processes of AI systems can be opaque, making it challenging to understand how decisions are made. Ensuring accountability and transparency in AI systems is essential for building trust and addressing potential issues.
- **Safety and Control**: As AI systems become more advanced, ensuring their safety and control becomes increasingly important. This includes developing mechanisms to prevent unintended consequences, ensuring robustness against adversarial attacks, and managing the risks associated with autonomous systems.

Applications of Artificial Intelligence

AI technologies have diverse applications across various industries and sectors:

- **Healthcare**: AI is used in medical imaging analysis, drug discovery, personalized medicine, and patient monitoring. AI algorithms can assist in diagnosing diseases, predicting treatment outcomes, and optimizing healthcare delivery.
- **Finance**: AI applications in finance include algorithmic trading, fraud detection, credit scoring, and customer service. AI systems can analyze financial data, detect anomalies, and provide insights for investment decisions.

- **Transportation**: AI is integral to autonomous vehicles, traffic management, and route optimization. Self-driving cars use AI algorithms for perception, decision-making, and control, while AI systems improve transportation efficiency and safety.
- **Retail**: AI enhances customer experience through personalized recommendations, inventory management, and demand forecasting. AI-driven chatbots and virtual assistants assist with customer service and engagement.
- **Education**: AI applications in education include adaptive learning platforms, automated grading, and intelligent tutoring systems. AI can personalize learning experiences and provide feedback to students and educators.

Future Directions and Challenges

The future of AI is marked by ongoing research and development, with several emerging trends and challenges:

- **Advancements in AI Algorithms**: Continued research focuses on developing more efficient and scalable AI algorithms, including advancements in deep learning, reinforcement learning, and generative models.
- **Integration with Emerging Technologies**: AI is increasingly integrated with other technologies such as the Internet of Things (IoT), blockchain, and 5G. These integrations enable new applications and enhance the capabilities of AI systems.
- **Ethical and Regulatory Frameworks**: The development of ethical guidelines and regulatory frameworks for AI is crucial for addressing concerns related to bias, privacy, and safety. Collaborative efforts among policymakers, researchers, and industry stakeholders are essential for creating responsible AI practices.
- **Human-AI Collaboration**: The future of AI involves enhancing human-AI collaboration, where AI systems complement and augment human capabilities rather than replace them. This approach emphasizes the synergy between human intelligence and artificial intelligence.

Artificial Intelligence is a dynamic and rapidly evolving field with profound implications for society and industry. Understanding the fundamentals of AI, including its definitions, types, core components, and applications, provides a foundation for exploring its potential and addressing its challenges. As AI continues to advance, ongoing research, ethical considerations, and collaborative efforts will shape the future of this transformative technology. The integration of AI into various domains offers opportunities for innovation and improvement, while also necessitating careful attention to its broader impact on society.

2.1 Introduction to AI and Machine Learning

Artificial Intelligence (AI) and Machine Learning (ML) are among the most transformative technological advancements of the 21st century, reshaping industries, driving innovation, and influencing everyday life. Both concepts, while often used interchangeably, represent distinct but interrelated areas of computer science. AI encompasses a broad range of technologies and approaches aimed at creating intelligent systems capable of performing tasks that would normally require human intelligence. Machine Learning, a subset of AI, focuses specifically on the development of algorithms and statistical models that enable computers to learn from data and make decisions or predictions. This introduction explores the fundamentals of AI and ML, their relationship, core concepts, methodologies, applications, and the implications of their advancements.

The Relationship Between AI and ML

AI and ML are interrelated but distinct concepts. AI is the overarching field that encompasses various approaches to creating intelligent systems, while ML is a specific methodology used to achieve AI. In essence, ML provides the tools and techniques that enable AI systems to learn and adapt. Here’s a breakdown of their relationship:

- **AI**: Represents the broad goal of creating systems that exhibit intelligence. AI includes various approaches such as rule-based systems, expert systems, and knowledge-based systems, in addition to machine learning. The goal of AI is to create systems that can perform tasks requiring human-like cognition and decision-making.
- **ML**: A subset of AI that focuses specifically on using data and algorithms to train systems. ML algorithms analyze large volumes of data to identify patterns, make predictions, and improve performance over time. While ML is a key technique for achieving AI, AI encompasses other techniques and approaches beyond ML.

Core Concepts in AI

To understand AI, it’s essential to grasp several core concepts:

- **Intelligent Agents**: Intelligent agents are systems that perceive their environment, make decisions, and take actions to achieve specific goals. They can operate autonomously or semi-autonomously and adapt their behavior based on their experiences. Examples include autonomous vehicles, personal assistants, and recommendation systems.
- **Learning**: Learning is a fundamental aspect of AI that involves acquiring knowledge or skills through experience. Machine learning is a prominent method for achieving learning in AI systems, enabling them to improve their performance based on data.
- **Reasoning**: Reasoning involves using logic and inference to draw conclusions or make decisions. AI systems employ various reasoning techniques, such as rule-based reasoning, probabilistic reasoning, and symbolic reasoning, to handle complex tasks and make informed decisions.
- **Perception**: Perception refers to the ability of AI systems to interpret and understand sensory inputs, such as images, sounds, and text. Computer vision and natural language processing are key areas of AI that focus on perception, enabling systems to analyze visual and textual data.
- **Adaptation**: Adaptation involves modifying behavior or strategies based on new information or changing circumstances. AI systems can adapt by learning from new data, adjusting their algorithms, and improving their performance over time.

Core Concepts in Machine Learning

Machine Learning involves several core concepts that are crucial for understanding how it works:

- **Algorithms**: Algorithms are the mathematical and computational procedures used to process data and generate predictions or decisions. Common ML algorithms include linear regression, decision trees, support vector machines, and neural networks.
- **Models**: Models are representations of the learned patterns and relationships in data. An ML model is trained on a dataset to identify patterns and make predictions. Once trained, the model can be used to make predictions on new, unseen data.
- **Training and Testing**: The process of training involves using a dataset to teach an ML model to recognize patterns and make predictions. The dataset is typically divided into training and testing subsets. The training subset is used to build the model, while the testing subset evaluates the model's performance and generalization ability.
- **Features and Labels**: Features are the input variables or attributes used by an ML model to make predictions, while labels are the output variables or target values the model aims to predict.

For example, in a classification task, features might include age and income, while labels could be categories such as "high risk" or "low risk."

- **Overfitting and Underfitting**: Overfitting occurs when a model learns the training data too well, including noise and anomalies, leading to poor performance on new data. Underfitting occurs when a model is too simple to capture the underlying patterns in the data. Balancing between overfitting and underfitting is crucial for building effective ML models.

Types of Machine Learning

Machine Learning is typically categorized into three main types based on how models are trained and the nature of the learning task:

- **Supervised Learning**: In supervised learning, models are trained on labeled data, where each input is paired with a corresponding output. The goal is to learn a mapping from inputs to outputs based on this training data. Common supervised learning tasks include classification (e.g., spam detection) and regression (e.g., predicting house prices). Algorithms used in supervised learning include decision trees, support vector machines, and neural networks.
- **Unsupervised Learning**: Unsupervised learning involves training models on unlabeled data to identify patterns or groupings without predefined outcomes. The goal is to discover hidden structures or relationships in the data. Common unsupervised learning tasks include clustering (e.g., customer segmentation) and dimensionality reduction (e.g., principal component analysis). Algorithms used in unsupervised learning include k-means clustering and hierarchical clustering.
- **Reinforcement Learning**: Reinforcement learning focuses on training models to make decisions based on interactions with an environment. The model, known as an agent, learns to take actions that maximize cumulative rewards over time. Reinforcement learning is used in applications such as game playing, robotics, and autonomous driving. Key algorithms include Q-learning and deep Q-networks (DQN).

Key Techniques and Approaches in AI and ML

AI and ML encompass a variety of techniques and approaches that drive their functionality:

- **Neural Networks**: Neural networks are computational models inspired by the human brain's structure and function. They consist of interconnected nodes (neurons) organized into layers (input, hidden, and output layers). Neural networks are used in various ML tasks, including image recognition, natural language processing, and game playing.

- **Deep Learning**: Deep learning is a subset of ML that involves neural networks with many layers (deep neural networks). Deep learning models can automatically learn features and representations from raw data, enabling them to handle complex tasks such as speech recognition and image classification. Common deep learning architectures include convolutional neural networks (CNNs) and recurrent neural networks (RNNs).
- **Natural Language Processing (NLP)**: NLP is a field of AI focused on enabling machines to understand and generate human language. NLP techniques are used for tasks such as language translation, sentiment analysis, and text generation. Key approaches include tokenization, part-of-speech tagging, and named entity recognition.
- **Computer Vision**: Computer vision involves analyzing and interpreting visual information from images and videos. Techniques in computer vision include object detection, image segmentation, and facial recognition. Deep learning models, particularly CNNs, have revolutionized computer vision by achieving state-of-the-art performance in various tasks.
- **Optimization Algorithms**: Optimization algorithms are used to improve the performance of ML models by adjusting their parameters. Common optimization techniques include gradient descent, stochastic gradient descent, and Adam optimization. These algorithms help in finding the best parameters that minimize the error or loss function of the model.

Applications of AI and Machine Learning

AI and ML have widespread applications across various industries and sectors:

- **Healthcare**: AI and ML are used in medical imaging analysis, drug discovery, disease diagnosis, and personalized treatment. AI-powered systems can assist in detecting anomalies in medical scans, predicting patient outcomes, and recommending treatments based on individual patient data.
- **Finance**: In finance, AI and ML are employed for algorithmic trading, fraud detection, credit scoring, and risk management. AI systems can analyze financial data, detect fraudulent transactions, and provide insights for investment decisions.
- **Retail**: AI and ML enhance customer experience through personalized recommendations, inventory management, and demand forecasting. AI-driven chatbots and virtual assistants assist

with customer service and engagement, while ML algorithms optimize inventory and supply chain operations.

- **Transportation**: AI and ML are integral to autonomous vehicles, traffic management, and route optimization. Self-driving cars use AI algorithms for perception, decision-making, and control, while AI systems improve transportation efficiency and safety.
- **Education**: In education, AI and ML are used for adaptive learning platforms, automated grading, and intelligent tutoring systems. AI can personalize learning experiences, provide feedback to students, and support educators in delivering effective instruction.

Ethical and Societal Implications

The advancement of AI and ML raises important ethical and societal considerations:

- **Bias and Fairness**: AI and ML systems can perpetuate biases present in training data, leading to unfair or discriminatory outcomes. Addressing bias and ensuring fairness require diverse data representation, careful design, and ongoing evaluation.
- **Privacy**: AI applications that involve data collection and analysis can pose privacy concerns, particularly when dealing with sensitive personal information. Data protection regulations, such as the General Data Protection Regulation (GDPR), play a critical role in safeguarding individuals' privacy.
- **Job Displacement**: The automation of tasks through AI and ML can lead to job displacement and changes in the labor market. Addressing the impact on employment requires strategies for workforce retraining and adaptation to new roles created by technological advancements.
- **Accountability and Transparency**: The decision-making processes of AI systems can be opaque, making it challenging to understand how decisions are made. Ensuring accountability and transparency in AI systems is essential for building trust and addressing potential issues.
- **Safety and Control**: As AI and ML systems become more advanced, ensuring their safety and control becomes increasingly important. This includes developing mechanisms to prevent unintended consequences, ensuring robustness against adversarial attacks, and managing the risks associated with autonomous systems.

Artificial Intelligence and Machine Learning represent transformative advancements that are reshaping technology, industry, and society. Understanding the fundamentals of AI and ML, including their definitions, core concepts, techniques, and applications, provides a foundation for exploring their potential and addressing their challenges. As AI and ML continue to evolve, ongoing research, ethical considerations, and collaborative efforts will play a crucial role in shaping their future impact. The integration of AI and ML into various domains offers opportunities for innovation and improvement, while also necessitating careful attention to their broader implications.

2.2 Types of Machine Learning: Supervised, Unsupervised, and Reinforcement Learning

Machine Learning (ML) is a dynamic field of artificial intelligence (AI) that focuses on developing algorithms and statistical models that allow computers to perform specific tasks without being explicitly programmed. The core idea of ML is to enable systems to learn from data and improve their performance over time. Machine learning can be categorized into three primary types based on the nature of the learning process and the type of data used: supervised learning, unsupervised learning, and reinforcement learning. Each type has unique characteristics, methodologies, applications, and challenges. This comprehensive exploration delves into these three types of machine learning, providing an in-depth understanding of their principles, techniques, and real-world applications.

Supervised Learning Definition and Overview

Supervised learning is a type of machine learning where the algorithm is trained on a labeled dataset. In this context, "labeled" means that each training example in the dataset is paired with an output label or target value. The goal of supervised learning is to learn a mapping from inputs to outputs that can make accurate predictions or classifications on new, unseen data.

Key Concepts

- **Training Data and Labels**: In supervised learning, the training data consists of input-output pairs. The input data, or features, represent the attributes of the data point, while the output data, or labels, represent the desired outcome or classification. For example, in a spam detection system, the input data could be email text, and the label would be whether the email is spam or not.
- **Loss Function**: A loss function quantifies the difference between the predicted output of the model and the actual output (label). It serves as a measure of how well the model is performing. Common loss functions include mean squared error (MSE) for regression tasks and cross-entropy loss for classification tasks.

- **Model Training**: During training, the model adjusts its parameters to minimize the loss function. This process is often performed using optimization algorithms such as gradient descent, which iteratively updates the model's parameters to reduce the loss.
- **Evaluation Metrics**: Supervised learning models are evaluated using various metrics depending on the type of task. For classification tasks, metrics include accuracy, precision, recall, and F1-score. For regression tasks, metrics such as mean absolute error (MAE), root mean squared error (RMSE), and R-squared are commonly used.

Types of Supervised Learning

- **Classification**: Classification tasks involve predicting discrete labels or categories. For example, classifying emails into "spam" or "not spam" is a classification task. Common algorithms used for classification include logistic regression, decision trees, random forests, support vector machines (SVMs), and neural networks.
- **Regression**: Regression tasks involve predicting continuous numerical values. For example, predicting house prices based on features such as size, location, and number of bedrooms is a regression task. Common regression algorithms include linear regression, polynomial regression, and ridge regression.

Applications

- **Healthcare**: Supervised learning is used for diagnosing diseases based on medical images, predicting patient outcomes, and personalized treatment recommendations. For example, models can be trained to classify MRI scans as indicating a particular disease.
- **Finance**: In finance, supervised learning is applied to credit scoring, fraud detection, and algorithmic trading. For instance, credit scoring models predict the likelihood of a borrower defaulting on a loan based on historical data.
- **Marketing**: Supervised learning helps in customer segmentation, predicting customer behavior, and targeted advertising. Models can be trained to predict which customers are likely to respond to a marketing campaign.

Unsupervised Learning Definition and Overview

Unsupervised learning is a type of machine learning where the algorithm is trained on an unlabeled dataset. Unlike supervised learning, there are no predefined output labels or target values in the training data. The goal of unsupervised learning is to explore and identify patterns, structures, or relationships within the data without prior knowledge of the outcomes.

Key Concepts

- **Clustering**: Clustering is a common unsupervised learning task that involves grouping similar data points together based on their features. The goal is to discover natural groupings within the data. Common clustering algorithms include k-means clustering, hierarchical clustering, and DBSCAN.
- **Dimensionality Reduction**: Dimensionality reduction involves reducing the number of features in the dataset while retaining essential information. This technique is used to simplify data, visualize high-dimensional data, and improve model performance. Common dimensionality reduction algorithms include principal component analysis (PCA) and t-distributed stochastic neighbor embedding (t-SNE).
- **Association Rules**: Association rule learning is used to identify relationships or associations between different items in a dataset. For example, in market basket analysis, association rules can reveal items frequently purchased together. The Apriori algorithm is a well-known method for association rule mining.

Types of Unsupervised Learning

- **Clustering**: Clustering algorithms group data points into clusters based on similarity. Each cluster represents a group of similar data points, with the goal of maximizing intra-cluster similarity and minimizing inter-cluster similarity. Clustering is used in various applications, such as customer segmentation and anomaly detection.
- **Dimensionality Reduction**: Dimensionality reduction techniques are used to reduce the number of features in a dataset while preserving its structure and relationships. This helps in visualizing high-dimensional data and improving the efficiency of machine learning algorithms. Dimensionality reduction is used in data preprocessing and feature extraction.

Applications

- **Market Analysis**: Unsupervised learning is used to segment customers based on purchasing behavior, identify market trends, and perform market basket analysis. For example, clustering algorithms can group customers with similar buying patterns.

- **Anomaly Detection**: Unsupervised learning helps in identifying unusual or rare events in data, such as fraud detection in financial transactions or detecting network intrusions. Anomalies are data points that deviate significantly from the norm.
- **Data Visualization**: Dimensionality reduction techniques are used to visualize high-dimensional data in lower-dimensional spaces. This helps in understanding data distributions and relationships. For instance, PCA can reduce the dimensionality of gene expression data for visualization.

Reinforcement Learning Definition and Overview

Reinforcement Learning (RL) is a type of machine learning where an agent learns to make decisions by interacting with an environment. The agent takes actions to maximize cumulative rewards over time based on feedback from the environment. Unlike supervised learning, RL does not rely on labeled data but instead learns through trial and error.

Key Concepts

- **Agent and Environment**: In reinforcement learning, the agent is the decision-maker that interacts with the environment. The environment provides feedback in the form of rewards or penalties based on the agent's actions. The agent's goal is to learn a policy that maximizes the cumulative reward.
- **Reward Signal**: The reward signal provides feedback to the agent about the quality of its actions. Positive rewards encourage the agent to take certain actions, while negative rewards discourage it. The agent uses this feedback to adjust its behavior and improve its performance.
- **Policy**: A policy is a strategy used by the agent to determine which actions to take in different states of the environment. The policy can be deterministic (always choosing the same action for a given state) or stochastic (choosing actions probabilistically).
- **Value Function**: The value function estimates the expected cumulative reward that can be obtained from a given state or state-action pair. It helps the agent evaluate the long-term benefits of its actions. Common value functions include state-value functions and action-value functions.

Types of Reinforcement Learning

- **Model-Free Methods**: Model-free methods do not require a model of the environment and learn directly from interactions. These methods include Q-learning, where the agent learns the action-value function to determine the best actions, and policy gradient methods, which optimize the policy directly.

- **Model-Based Methods**: Model-based methods involve learning a model of the environment and using it to make decisions. The agent builds a model to predict the consequences of actions and uses this model to plan and optimize its behavior.

Applications

- **Game Playing**: Reinforcement learning has been successfully applied to game playing, with notable examples including AlphaGo, which defeated human champions in the game of Go. RL algorithms learn optimal strategies by playing games and receiving feedback.
- **Robotics**: In robotics, RL is used to train robots to perform complex tasks such as manipulation, navigation, and control. Robots learn to interact with their environment and improve their performance through trial and error.
- **Autonomous Vehicles**: RL is used in autonomous vehicles to develop driving policies that maximize safety and efficiency. The vehicle learns to navigate complex environments, make decisions, and respond to changing conditions.

Comparing Supervised, Unsupervised, and Reinforcement Learning

Data Requirements: Supervised learning requires labeled data for training, while unsupervised learning works with unlabeled data. Reinforcement learning does not rely on labeled data but learns from interactions with the environment.

Learning Process: In supervised learning, the model learns a mapping from inputs to outputs based on labeled examples. In unsupervised learning, the model discovers patterns and structures in the data without predefined labels. In reinforcement learning, the agent learns by interacting with the environment and receiving feedback in the form of rewards.

Applications: Supervised learning is commonly used in classification and regression tasks. Unsupervised learning is applied to clustering, dimensionality reduction, and association rule mining. Reinforcement learning is used in decision-making tasks such as game playing, robotics, and autonomous vehicles.

Challenges: Supervised learning requires high-quality labeled data, which can be expensive and time-consuming to obtain. Unsupervised learning faces challenges related to the interpretability of results and the lack of ground truth. Reinforcement learning can be computationally intensive and requires careful tuning of rewards and exploration strategies.

Machine learning encompasses a diverse range of techniques and approaches that enable computers to learn from data and improve their performance over time. Supervised learning, unsupervised learning, and reinforcement learning each represent distinct methodologies with unique characteristics, applications, and challenges. Understanding these types of machine learning provides a foundation for leveraging their capabilities and addressing the specific needs of various domains and tasks. As machine learning continues to advance, these foundational techniques will remain integral to the development of intelligent systems and the exploration of new frontiers in AI.

2.3 Overview of AI Techniques Relevant to Health Assessment

Artificial Intelligence (AI) is revolutionizing health assessment by providing advanced tools and methodologies that enhance the accuracy, efficiency, and personalization of healthcare services. AI techniques span across machine learning, natural language processing (NLP), computer vision, and expert systems, each contributing to various aspects of health assessment. This comprehensive overview explores these AI techniques in detail, highlighting their applications and impacts on healthcare.

Machine Learning in Health Assessment

Machine learning (ML) involves training algorithms to recognize patterns and make predictions based on data. In health assessment, ML techniques are instrumental in analyzing large datasets to support clinical decision-making, predict patient outcomes, and identify disease risks.

Supervised Learning

Supervised learning algorithms are trained using labeled data where the outcome is known. Common supervised learning methods in health assessment include:

- **Logistic Regression:** Utilized for binary classification tasks, such as predicting the likelihood of a disease (e.g., whether a patient has diabetes or not). It helps in understanding the relationship between patient features and disease outcomes.

- **Decision Trees and Random Forests:** Decision trees model decisions based on various conditions and are useful for tasks such as risk stratification. Random forests, an ensemble of decision trees, improve prediction accuracy and robustness by aggregating results from multiple trees.
- **Support Vector Machines (SVM):** SVMs are effective in high-dimensional spaces, making them suitable for tasks like cancer diagnosis where features are numerous. They work by finding the optimal hyperplane that separates different classes.

Unsupervised Learning

Unsupervised learning techniques are applied when the outcome labels are not available, helping to uncover hidden patterns within the data:

- **Clustering Algorithms (e.g., K-Means, Hierarchical Clustering):** These algorithms group patients with similar characteristics or disease phenotypes. For instance, clustering can identify subtypes of cancer or patterns in patient responses to treatment.
- **Dimensionality Reduction (e.g., Principal Component Analysis, t-SNE):** These techniques reduce the number of features in a dataset while retaining essential information. They are valuable in genomic studies and visualizing complex health data.

Reinforcement Learning

Reinforcement learning focuses on training algorithms to make a series of decisions by learning from the outcomes of previous actions. In health assessment, it can optimize personalized treatment plans by continuously learning from patient responses and adjusting strategies accordingly.

Ensemble Learning

Ensemble learning combines predictions from multiple models to improve overall performance. Techniques such as boosting, bagging, and stacking are employed to enhance predictive accuracy. For example, ensemble methods can integrate various diagnostic models to provide a more reliable assessment of disease risk.

Natural Language Processing (NLP) in Health Assessment

Natural Language Processing (NLP) is a branch of AI that enables computers to understand and interpret human language. In healthcare, NLP techniques are used to extract valuable information from unstructured text data, such as clinical notes and EHRs.

Named Entity Recognition (NER)

NER identifies and classifies key entities in text, such as diseases, medications, and patient information. This technique automates the extraction of critical data from clinical narratives, aiding in the organization and analysis of patient records.

Sentiment Analysis

Sentiment analysis evaluates patient feedback, reviews, and other text data to assess sentiments and emotions. This can provide insights into patient satisfaction, adherence to treatment, and mental health status, contributing to better patient care and engagement.

Text Classification

Text classification algorithms categorize medical texts into predefined categories. For instance, they can classify clinical notes into different types of conditions or treatments. This helps in organizing and retrieving relevant information efficiently, enhancing clinical workflows.

Relation Extraction

Relation extraction identifies and establishes relationships between entities mentioned in text. In healthcare, it can link diseases with symptoms, treatments, or outcomes, facilitating a deeper understanding of disease mechanisms and patient interactions.

Question Answering Systems

Question answering systems leverage NLP to automatically answer queries posed in natural language. These systems can provide clinicians with rapid access to medical knowledge, research findings, and patient information, supporting informed decision-making.

Computer Vision in Health Assessment

Computer vision techniques enable machines to interpret and analyze visual information from medical images. These techniques are pivotal in diagnostics, treatment planning, and monitoring.

Image Classification

Image classification algorithms categorize medical images into various classes based on their content. For example, these algorithms can differentiate between benign and malignant tumors in mammograms or classify types of retinal diseases from fundus images. Accurate image classification supports early diagnosis and effective treatment planning.

Object Detection

Object detection algorithms locate and identify specific objects within an image. In medical imaging, this includes identifying tumors, lesions, or other abnormalities. For instance, object detection can be used to pinpoint cancerous regions in CT scans or MRI images.

Image Segmentation

Image segmentation involves dividing an image into multiple segments or regions, each corresponding to different structures or abnormalities. This technique is crucial for delineating anatomical structures or pathological areas in medical images, such as segmenting brain regions in MRI scans.

Image Registration

Image registration aligns multiple images of the same patient taken at different times or using different modalities. This is essential for tracking disease progression, planning surgical interventions, and integrating data from various imaging sources.

Expert Systems in Health Assessment

Expert systems are AI applications that simulate human expertise to make decisions and solve complex problems. In health assessment, expert systems use knowledge bases and inference engines to support clinical decision-making.

Rule-Based Systems

Rule-based expert systems apply predefined rules to clinical data to generate recommendations or diagnoses. For instance, a rule-based system might use a set of clinical guidelines to suggest treatment options based on patient symptoms and medical history.

Knowledge Representation

Knowledge representation involves encoding medical knowledge into a structured format that can be used by expert systems. This includes creating ontologies and knowledge graphs that represent relationships between diseases, symptoms, treatments, and patient characteristics.

Diagnostic Support Systems

Diagnostic support systems assist clinicians by providing diagnostic suggestions based on patient data. These systems leverage a combination of rule-based reasoning, machine learning models, and medical knowledge to enhance diagnostic accuracy and reduce errors.

Decision Support Systems

Decision support systems aid clinicians in making complex decisions by integrating patient data, clinical guidelines, and evidence-based research. These systems help in developing personalized treatment plans, evaluating potential interventions, and optimizing patient outcomes.

The integration of AI techniques into health assessment represents a transformative shift in healthcare, offering powerful tools to enhance diagnostic accuracy, personalize treatment, and improve patient outcomes. Machine learning, natural language processing, computer vision, and expert systems each play a crucial role in advancing the capabilities of health assessment. By leveraging these technologies, healthcare professionals can gain deeper insights into patient health, streamline clinical workflows, and ultimately deliver better care. As AI continues to evolve, its impact on health assessment is expected to grow, driving innovations that will further enhance the quality and efficiency of healthcare services.

3. Data Collection and Preprocessing

Data collection and preprocessing are fundamental stages in the data science pipeline that play a critical role in ensuring the accuracy, reliability, and relevance of data used for analysis and machine learning. Data collection involves gathering information from diverse sources to create a comprehensive dataset. This process includes selecting appropriate data sources, such as surveys, sensors, web scraping, and databases, and ensuring the data is representative of the problem being studied. Effective data collection must address challenges such as ensuring data accuracy, managing privacy concerns, and dealing with varying data formats and structures. Following data collection, preprocessing transforms raw data into a format suitable for analysis. This stage includes several key activities: data cleaning, where missing values are handled, duplicates are removed, and errors are corrected; data transformation, which involves normalizing numerical values, encoding categorical variables, and aggregating data to a consistent format; data integration, which combines data from multiple sources and aligns disparate data schemas; and data reduction, which focuses on techniques like dimensionality reduction to simplify the dataset without losing critical information. Data preprocessing also involves addressing class imbalances and ensuring that the data is representative of the real-world scenarios it aims to model. The primary goals of preprocessing are to improve data quality, enhance usability, and ensure consistency across datasets. Challenges during this phase include managing large volumes of data, addressing discrepancies between data sources, and maintaining data privacy and security. By meticulously handling data collection and preprocessing, organizations can ensure that their datasets are robust and well-prepared for analysis, leading to more accurate insights, effective decision-making, and successful deployment of machine learning models.

3.1 Types of Data Collected from Transformers

Transformers are crucial components in electrical power systems, converting voltages to levels suitable for transmission and distribution. Effective monitoring and maintenance of transformers are essential to ensure their reliable operation and longevity. The types of data collected from transformers cover a broad spectrum of operational and condition metrics, including temperature, vibration, oil quality, electrical parameters, and more. This comprehensive overview explores each type of data in detail, explaining its significance, measurement techniques, and the insights it provides for transformer management.

Temperature Data

Temperature monitoring is vital for ensuring that transformers operate within safe thermal limits. Excessive heat can lead to insulation degradation, reduced efficiency, and even catastrophic failures.

Winding Temperature

- **Purpose:** Transformer windings, composed of conductive materials like copper or aluminum, generate heat during operation. Excessive winding temperature can signal overloading, inadequate cooling, or insulation problems. Maintaining the winding temperature within specified limits helps prevent overheating and extends the transformer's lifespan.
- **Measurement Techniques:**
    - **Resistance Temperature Detectors (RTDs):** RTDs offer accurate temperature measurements based on the change in electrical resistance of a metal with temperature. They are often installed in or near transformer windings to monitor temperature continuously.
    - **Thermocouples:** These sensors measure temperature through the voltage produced at the junction of two different metals. They are suitable for high-temperature environments and provide real-time data.
    - **Fiber Optic Sensors:** Utilizing light transmission through optical fibers, these sensors can measure temperature without conducting electricity, making them ideal for high-voltage transformers.

Ambient Temperature

- **Purpose:** Ambient temperature influences the efficiency of the transformer's cooling system. High ambient temperatures can reduce cooling effectiveness and increase the risk of overheating.
- **Measurement Techniques:**
    - **Thermometers:** Basic instruments that provide direct temperature readings of the surrounding environment.
    - **Digital Temperature Sensors:** Provide continuous, real-time ambient temperature data, often integrated into broader monitoring systems.

Oil Temperature

- **Purpose:** Transformer oil acts as both an insulator and coolant. Monitoring oil temperature is crucial for assessing the efficiency of the cooling system and detecting potential issues such as overheating.
- **Measurement Techniques:**
    - **Thermocouples:** Measure oil temperature directly by immersion in the oil.
    - **RTDs:** Offer precise temperature measurements for monitoring the thermal condition of the oil.

Vibration Data

Vibration monitoring is critical for detecting mechanical issues and ensuring the mechanical integrity of the transformer and associated components.

Core Vibration

- **Purpose:** Vibrations in the core can indicate problems such as loose laminations, core movement, or mechanical resonance. Excessive vibrations can lead to operational inefficiencies and potential damage.
- **Measurement Techniques:**
    - **Accelerometers:** Measure the acceleration of vibrations and can be mounted on the transformer core to capture data.
    - **Vibration Sensors:** Provide detailed measurements of vibration patterns and amplitudes.

Bearing Vibration

- **Purpose:** Bearings, especially in cooling fans or pumps, are prone to wear and tear. Monitoring bearing vibrations helps in detecting early signs of mechanical failure, which can prevent operational disruptions.
- **Measurement Techniques:**
    - **Accelerometers:** Installed on bearing housings to monitor vibrations and identify issues such as imbalance or misalignment.
    - **Vibration Monitoring Systems:** Provide real-time data and alerts for abnormal vibration patterns, facilitating early intervention.

Structural Vibration

- **Purpose:** Monitoring the vibrations of the transformer's structural components helps in identifying mechanical stress, misalignment, or other structural issues that might affect performance and safety.
- **Measurement Techniques:**
  - **Accelerometers and Vibration Sensors:** Installed on various structural parts of the transformer to monitor vibrations and ensure structural integrity.

Oil Quality Data

Oil quality is a critical aspect of transformer maintenance, as it affects both insulation performance and cooling efficiency. Regular analysis of oil quality helps in detecting issues before they lead to serious problems.

Dissolved Gas Analysis (DGA)

- **Purpose:** DGA measures the concentration of gases dissolved in transformer oil. Elevated levels of gases such as hydrogen, methane, and ethane can indicate faults such as overheating, arcing, or insulation breakdown.
- **Measurement Techniques:**
  - **Gas Chromatographs:** Analyze the composition of dissolved gases by separating them based on their chemical properties.
  - **Online DGA Units:** Continuously monitor and analyze gas levels in real-time, providing early warnings of potential issues.

Moisture Content

- **Purpose:** Excess moisture in transformer oil can reduce its insulating properties, leading to increased risk of electrical faults and reduced transformer efficiency.
- **Measurement Techniques:**
  - **Moisture Sensors:** Measure the amount of water present in the oil, often using capacitive or resistive techniques.
  - **Coulometric and Capacitive Sensors:** Common methods for accurately assessing moisture levels in the oil.

Acid Number

- **Purpose:** The acid number of transformer oil indicates the level of acidity, which can affect the oil's insulating properties and contribute to degradation. Monitoring the acid number helps in assessing the condition of the oil.
- **Measurement Techniques:**
  - **Titration Methods:** Determine the acid number through chemical reactions with a known base.
  - **Automated Testers:** Provide rapid analysis of the oil's acid number, enabling timely decision-making.

Dielectric Strength

- **Purpose:** The dielectric strength of transformer oil measures its ability to withstand electrical stress without breaking down. A decrease in dielectric strength indicates deteriorating insulation quality.
- **Measurement Techniques:**
  - **Dielectric Testers:** Apply a high voltage to the oil and measure the breakdown voltage to determine its dielectric strength.

Electrical Data

Electrical parameters provide insights into the operational performance of the transformer and help in ensuring it operates within its designed specifications.

Voltage Levels

- **Purpose:** Monitoring input and output voltage levels ensures the transformer operates within its specified voltage range, preventing potential damage or inefficiency.
- **Measurement Techniques:**
  - **Voltage Sensors:** Measure the electrical voltages on the primary and secondary sides of the transformer.
  - **Multimeters and Voltage Meters:** Provide periodic checks and calibrations for accurate voltage measurements.

Current Levels

- **Purpose:** Measuring current levels helps in assessing the load on the transformer and detecting potential overload conditions.
- **Measurement Techniques:**
    - **Current Transformers:** Measure the current flowing through the transformer windings and provide accurate readings.
    - **Clamp Meters:** Allow for non-intrusive measurements of current levels.

Power Factor

- **Purpose:** The power factor indicates how effectively the transformer converts electrical power into useful work. A low power factor can signal inefficiencies or potential issues that need addressing.
- **Measurement Techniques:**
    - **Power Factor Meters:** Measure the phase difference between voltage and current to determine the power factor.
    - **Power Quality Analyzers:** Provide detailed power factor measurements along with other electrical parameters, offering a comprehensive view of transformer performance.

Harmonic Distortion

- **Purpose:** Harmonic distortion can affect the transformer's performance and cause overheating. Monitoring harmonic distortion helps in identifying electrical quality issues and ensuring efficient operation.
- **Measurement Techniques:**
    - **Harmonic Analyzers:** Measure the levels of harmonic distortion in electrical signals, helping in diagnosing issues related to power quality.
    - **Power Quality Meters:** Offer a comprehensive analysis of harmonic content and other electrical characteristics.

Load Data

Load data provides insights into the operational patterns and performance of the transformer, aiding in capacity planning and maintenance scheduling.

Load Profile

- **Purpose:** Analyzing the load profile helps in understanding the transformer's operational patterns, identifying peak loads, and planning for future capacity needs.
- **Measurement Techniques:**
    - **Load Meters:** Record the varying load levels on the transformer over time.
    - **Data Loggers:** Capture and store load data, providing a detailed view of usage patterns and trends.

Load Cycles

- **Purpose:** Tracking load cycles provides insights into the transformer's usage patterns and helps in predicting maintenance needs based on load variations and operational demands.
- **Measurement Techniques:**
    - **Load Monitoring Systems:** Track the number and intensity of load cycles, offering insights into operational stress and maintenance requirements.
    - **Data Collection Software:** Analyzes load cycle data to identify patterns and predict future maintenance needs.

Insulation Data

Insulation data is critical for assessing the condition of the transformer's insulation system and preventing potential electrical failures.

Insulation Resistance

- **Purpose:** Monitoring insulation resistance helps assess the health of the transformer's insulation system. Low resistance can indicate potential breakdowns or degradation.
- **Measurement Techniques:**
    - **Insulation Resistance Testers:** Measure the resistance of insulation to electrical currents, providing insights into its condition.

  - **Megohmmeters:** Measure high resistance values and assess the insulation's effectiveness.

Power Factor of Insulation

- **Purpose:** The power factor of insulation provides an indication of its condition and effectiveness. A low power factor can signal insulation degradation or issues.
- **Measurement Techniques:**
  - **Power Factor Testers:** Assess the insulation's power factor, offering insights into its health and effectiveness.
  - **Dissipation Factor Measurements:** Evaluate the insulation's performance and condition.

Other Operational Data

Additional operational data helps in managing the overall performance and maintenance of transformers and associated systems.

Cooling System Performance

- **Purpose:** Ensuring the cooling system operates effectively is essential for maintaining the transformer's temperature and preventing overheating.
- **Measurement Techniques:**
  - **Cooling Fan and Pump Monitors:** Track the performance and efficiency of cooling systems.
  - **Temperature Sensors:** Monitor the temperature of cooling fluids and systems to ensure proper operation.

Circuit Breaker Status

- **Purpose:** Monitoring the status of circuit breakers ensures they function correctly and can protect the transformer from faults and overloads.
- **Measurement Techniques:**
  - **Breaker Monitors:** Track the operational status and performance of circuit breakers.

  - **Protective Relay Systems:** Provide real-time status updates and alerts for circuit breaker functionality.

Maintenance Records

- **Purpose:** Maintaining detailed records of maintenance activities helps manage the transformer's lifecycle and plan for future maintenance and repairs.
- **Measurement Techniques:**
  - **Maintenance Management Systems:** Record and manage details of inspections, repairs, and replacements.
  - **Automated Tracking Systems:** Facilitate the scheduling and tracking of maintenance activities, ensuring timely upkeep.

The data collected from transformers encompass a wide range of parameters, including temperature, vibration, oil quality, electrical metrics, and more. Each type of data provides valuable insights into the transformer's condition and performance, helping operators detect potential issues, optimize performance, and plan maintenance effectively. By systematically monitoring and analyzing these data points, utilities and maintenance teams can ensure the reliable operation of transformers, enhance system efficiency, and extend the equipment's lifespan.

3.2 Data Acquisition Methods and Sensors

In the realm of transformer monitoring and maintenance, accurate and timely data acquisition is crucial for ensuring operational reliability and efficiency. Transformers, as essential components in electrical power systems, require detailed monitoring of various parameters such as temperature, vibration, oil quality, and electrical performance. This comprehensive overview explores the methods and sensors used for data acquisition in transformers, highlighting their principles, applications, advantages, and limitations.

Temperature Data Acquisition - ***Methods of Temperature Measurement***

Temperature monitoring in transformers is vital for preventing overheating, ensuring proper operation, and extending equipment life. Temperature data acquisition can be achieved using both direct and non-contact methods.

- **Direct Contact Sensors:** These sensors are placed in direct contact with transformer components or fluids. They provide precise measurements and are typically used for critical temperature points.
- **Non-Contact Sensors:** These sensors measure temperature from a distance using methods like infrared radiation or fiber optics. They are useful for high-voltage environments or where physical contact is impractical.

Types of Temperature Sensors

Resistance Temperature Detectors (RTDs)

- **Principle:** RTDs operate on the principle that the electrical resistance of certain metals (commonly platinum) changes predictably with temperature. The resistance increases as temperature rises, and this change is measured to determine the temperature.
- **Applications:** RTDs are widely used for measuring winding and oil temperatures in transformers due to their high accuracy and stability.
- **Advantages:** RTDs offer high precision, good repeatability, and stability over a wide temperature range. They are well-suited for applications requiring long-term accuracy.
- **Limitations:** RTDs can be more expensive than other sensors and may require careful calibration and maintenance.

Thermocouples

- **Principle:** Thermocouples consist of two different metals joined at one end. When this junction is heated or cooled, it produces a voltage proportional to the temperature difference, which is measured to determine temperature.
- **Applications:** Thermocouples are used for measuring both winding and ambient temperatures. They are especially useful in high-temperature environments.
- **Advantages:** They are durable, cost-effective, and capable of measuring a broad temperature range. Thermocouples also have a fast response time.
- **Limitations:** They may be less accurate than RTDs and can drift over time, requiring periodic calibration.

Fiber Optic Sensors

- **Principle:** Fiber optic sensors use the principles of light transmission through optical fibers. Temperature changes affect the properties of light traveling through the fibers, allowing for precise temperature measurement.
- **Applications:** These sensors are used in high-voltage environments and for distributed temperature sensing along transformer components.
- **Advantages:** Fiber optic sensors offer high accuracy, immunity to electromagnetic interference, and the ability to measure temperature at multiple points simultaneously.
- **Limitations:** They can be expensive and complex to install and maintain.

Vibration Data Acquisition

Methods of Vibration Measurement

Vibration monitoring helps in detecting mechanical issues such as imbalances, misalignments, and wear. Data acquisition methods include both direct and remote measurement techniques.

- **Direct Measurement:** Vibration sensors are mounted directly on transformer components to capture real-time vibration data.
- **Remote Measurement:** Wireless or remote sensors transmit vibration data to central monitoring systems, reducing the need for physical access to the transformer.

Types of Vibration Sensors

Accelerometers

- **Principle:** Accelerometers measure acceleration forces caused by vibrations. They detect changes in motion and convert them into electrical signals, providing information on vibration magnitude and frequency.
- **Applications:** Commonly used for monitoring core and bearing vibrations. They help in diagnosing mechanical issues and assessing operational health.
- **Advantages:** Accelerometers offer high sensitivity, a broad range of vibration frequencies, and can be installed in various orientations. They are effective for detecting both low and high-frequency vibrations.

- **Limitations:** They can be sensitive to environmental conditions and may require periodic calibration.

Proximity Probes

- **Principle:** Proximity probes measure the displacement and vibrations of rotating machinery by detecting the distance between the probe and the rotating part. They provide information on shaft movements and vibrations.
- **Applications:** Used for monitoring shaft vibrations and displacements in transformers and associated machinery.
- **Advantages:** High accuracy in measuring shaft movement and vibrations, suitable for high-speed applications.
- **Limitations:** Proximity probes can be sensitive to installation conditions and require precise alignment.

Vibration Monitors

- **Principle:** Vibration monitors combine multiple sensors and signal processing algorithms to provide a comprehensive analysis of vibration data. They often include features like frequency analysis and trend monitoring.
- **Applications:** Used for continuous monitoring of vibration levels and trends in transformers and related equipment.
- **Advantages:** Provides real-time analysis, trend monitoring, and can alert operators to potential issues.
- **Limitations:** Can be complex to configure and may require regular maintenance and calibration.

Oil Quality Data Acquisition

Oil quality monitoring is essential for assessing the condition of the transformer's insulation and cooling systems. Various parameters are measured to ensure the oil's effectiveness and safety.

Dissolved Gas Analysis (DGA)

- **Principle:** DGA measures the concentration of gases dissolved in transformer oil. Elevated levels of gases like hydrogen, methane, and ethane indicate potential issues such as overheating, arcing, or insulation breakdown.
- **Applications:** Used for detecting faults and assessing the condition of transformer oil.
- **Advantages:** Provides early detection of internal faults and helps in diagnosing the nature of the fault.
- **Limitations:** Requires periodic sampling and analysis, which can be time-consuming and may involve some delay in detecting issues.

Moisture Content Measurement

- **Principle:** Moisture sensors measure the amount of water present in transformer oil. Excess moisture can reduce the oil's insulating properties and increase the risk of electrical faults.
- **Applications:** Essential for monitoring the health of transformer insulation and preventing potential failures.
- **Advantages:** Provides accurate measurements of moisture levels and helps in maintaining oil quality.
- **Limitations:** Sensors may require calibration and maintenance to ensure accuracy.

Acid Number Measurement

- **Principle:** The acid number of transformer oil indicates its level of acidity. High acid numbers can affect insulation quality and contribute to oil degradation.
- **Applications:** Used for assessing the condition of transformer oil and planning maintenance activities.
- **Advantages:** Provides insights into the aging and degradation of transformer oil.
- **Limitations:** Measurement may require periodic sampling and laboratory analysis.

Dielectric Strength Measurement

- **Principle:** Dielectric strength measures the oil's ability to resist electrical breakdown. It is an indicator of the oil's insulating properties and overall quality.
- **Applications:** Used to evaluate the insulation effectiveness of transformer oil.

- **Advantages:** Provides direct measurement of oil quality and insulation performance.
- **Limitations:** Testing may require specialized equipment and periodic sampling.

Electrical Data Acquisition

Monitoring electrical parameters is critical for assessing the operational performance of the transformer and ensuring it operates within specified limits.

Voltage Measurement

- **Principle:** Voltage sensors measure the electrical potential difference between two points. Monitoring voltage levels ensures that the transformer operates within its designed voltage range.
- **Applications:** Used for measuring input and output voltages to verify operational performance.
- **Advantages:** Provides real-time data on voltage levels and helps in identifying potential issues.
- **Limitations:** Requires accurate calibration and installation to ensure reliable measurements.

Current Measurement

- **Principle:** Current transformers and clamp meters measure the current flowing through the transformer windings. Monitoring current levels helps in detecting overload conditions.
- **Applications:** Essential for assessing load conditions and ensuring transformer operation within safe limits.
- **Advantages:** Provides accurate measurements of current levels and helps in identifying overloads.
- **Limitations:** Can be affected by external factors and may require periodic calibration.

Power Factor Measurement

- **Principle:** Power factor meters measure the phase difference between voltage and current, providing an indication of the efficiency of power conversion. A low power factor can signal inefficiencies.
- **Applications:** Used to assess the efficiency of transformer operation and detect potential issues.
- **Advantages:** Offers insights into operational efficiency and power quality.
- **Limitations:** Requires accurate measurement and analysis to provide meaningful results.

Harmonic Distortion Measurement

- **Principle:** Harmonic analyzers measure the presence of harmonics in the electrical signal. Harmonics can affect transformer performance and cause overheating.
- **Applications:** Used for analyzing power quality and identifying electrical disturbances.
- **Advantages:** Provides detailed analysis of harmonic content and helps in diagnosing power quality issues.
- **Limitations:** Can be complex to set up and interpret, requiring specialized knowledge.

Load Data Acquisition

Load data helps in understanding transformer usage patterns and planning maintenance activities.

Load Profiling

- **Principle:** Load meters and data loggers measure and record the varying load levels on the transformer. Analyzing load profiles helps in understanding operational patterns and planning capacity needs.
- **Applications:** Essential for load management and capacity planning.
- **Advantages:** Provides detailed insights into load variations and trends.
- **Limitations:** Requires accurate data collection and analysis for effective utilization.

Load Cycles Tracking

- **Principle:** Load monitoring systems track the number and intensity of load cycles, providing information on operational stress and maintenance needs.
- **Applications:** Used for predicting maintenance requirements based on load patterns.
- **Advantages:** Helps in identifying patterns and planning maintenance activities.
- **Limitations:** May require sophisticated monitoring systems and data analysis.

Insulation Data Acquisition

Insulation data is crucial for assessing the condition of the transformer's insulation system and preventing electrical failures.

Insulation Resistance Measurement

- **Principle:** Insulation resistance testers measure the resistance of insulation to electrical currents. Low resistance indicates potential breakdowns or degradation.
- **Applications:** Used for assessing the health of transformer insulation.
- **Advantages:** Provides direct measurement of insulation condition and helps in planning maintenance.
- **Limitations:** Requires periodic testing and calibration to ensure accuracy.

Power Factor of Insulation Measurement

- **Principle:** The power factor of insulation indicates its condition and effectiveness. A low power factor can signal insulation degradation.
- **Applications:** Essential for evaluating insulation performance and planning maintenance.
- **Advantages:** Provides insights into insulation quality and helps in identifying potential issues.
- **Limitations:** Requires accurate measurement and interpretation for meaningful results.

Data acquisition methods and sensors play a critical role in monitoring the performance and condition of transformers. By leveraging various sensors and measurement techniques, operators can obtain valuable insights into temperature, vibration, oil quality, electrical parameters, and more. This information helps in maintaining the reliability and efficiency of transformers, preventing potential failures, and optimizing maintenance practices. As technology advances, new sensors and data acquisition methods continue to enhance the ability to monitor and manage transformer systems effectively.

3.3 Data Cleaning and Preprocessing Techniques

Data cleaning and preprocessing are fundamental steps in the data analysis pipeline, especially when dealing with complex datasets like those from transformers in electrical systems. These processes ensure that data is accurate, consistent, and ready for analysis, which is crucial for reliable performance monitoring, predictive maintenance, and decision-making. This comprehensive guide delves into the techniques used for data cleaning and preprocessing, providing a detailed understanding of each method and its application.

Understanding the Importance of Data Cleaning and Preprocessing

Data Quality and Accuracy

Data cleaning and preprocessing address issues related to data quality and accuracy. Inaccurate or inconsistent data can lead to incorrect analysis, misinformed decisions, and unreliable predictions. Ensuring high-quality data is critical for effective transformer monitoring, as it directly impacts the reliability of maintenance decisions and system performance assessments.

Consistency and Standardization

Transformers generate data from various sensors and sources, often leading to inconsistencies in format, scale, and units. Preprocessing standardizes this data, making it uniform and easier to analyze. This step is crucial for integrating data from different sensors and systems, ensuring that all data is comparable and interpretable.

Noise Reduction and Outlier Detection

Sensor data can be noisy or contain outliers due to environmental factors, sensor malfunctions, or data transmission errors. Cleaning techniques help in reducing noise and identifying outliers, which improves the quality of the data and the accuracy of the subsequent analysis.

Data Cleaning Techniques - Handling Missing Data

Identification of Missing Data

- **Detecting Missing Values:** Missing data can manifest as null entries, empty fields, or placeholders (e.g., "NA", "UNKNOWN"). Identifying these entries is the first step in cleaning. Tools and functions in programming languages like Python (using Pandas' isnull() or isna() methods) or R (using is.na() function) can automate this process.
- **Patterns in Missing Data:** Analyzing patterns (e.g., if data is missing at random or systematically) can inform the choice of imputation or deletion strategies.

Imputation Techniques

- **Mean/Median Imputation:** This involves replacing missing values with the mean or median of the non-missing values. It's useful for numerical data where the distribution is assumed to be normal.
  - **Mean Imputation:** Used when the data is symmetrically distributed.
  - **Median Imputation:** Preferred for skewed distributions or when outliers are present, as the median is less affected by extreme values.
- **Interpolation:** This method estimates missing values based on existing data points. Common techniques include:
  - **Linear Interpolation:** Fills in missing values by drawing a straight line between known points. Suitable for data that changes steadily.
  - **Polynomial or Spline Interpolation:** Provides a smoother estimate by fitting a polynomial or spline curve through the data points. Useful for data with more complex patterns.
- **K-Nearest Neighbors (KNN) Imputation:** This method uses the values from the k-nearest neighbors (data points) to estimate missing values. It's effective in capturing the local structure of the data.
  - **Distance Metric:** KNN imputation depends on distance metrics like Euclidean or Manhattan distance to find similar neighbors.
  - **Choosing K:** The number of neighbors (k) is crucial and typically chosen based on cross-validation.
- **Predictive Modeling:** Machine learning models predict missing values based on other features. Common models include:
  - **Regression Models:** Simple linear regression or more complex models like ridge or lasso regression can predict missing values based on relationships with other variables.
  - **Decision Trees:** These models use decision rules to estimate missing values based on feature splits.

Deletion Methods

- **Listwise Deletion:** This approach removes any rows with missing values. It's straightforward but can lead to a significant loss of data, especially if missing data is prevalent.
  - **Pros:** Simple to implement.

    - **Cons:** Can lead to biased results if the missing data is not missing at random (MAR) or missing completely at random (MCAR).
- **Pairwise Deletion:** This method excludes missing values only in the analyses where they are needed, allowing for the use of all available data.
    - **Pros:** Retains more data for analysis.
    - **Cons:** Can lead to inconsistencies in results if missing values vary across different analyses.

Handling Outliers-*Detection of Outliers*

- **Statistical Methods:**
    - **Z-Scores:** Measures how many standard deviations a data point is from the mean. Values beyond a specified threshold (e.g., ±3) are considered outliers.
    - **Modified Z-Scores:** An adjustment of Z-scores that uses the median and median absolute deviation (MAD) for robustness against outliers.
- **Boxplots:** Visual representation of data distribution. Outliers are identified as points outside the "whiskers" of the boxplot, which represent the interquartile range (IQR).
- **IQR Method:** Calculates outliers based on the IQR, defined as Q3 - Q1 (where Q3 is the third quartile and Q1 is the first quartile). Data points outside 1.5 times the IQR from the quartiles are considered outliers.

Treatment of Outliers

- **Transformation:** Applying mathematical transformations to reduce the impact of outliers. Examples include:
    - **Log Transformation:** Useful for right-skewed distributions to compress the range of values.
    - **Square Root Transformation:** Suitable for moderate skewness and helps in stabilizing variance.
- **Winsorization:** Replaces outliers with the nearest value within a specified percentile range. This reduces the effect of extreme values while preserving data integrity.
- **Truncation:** Caps values at predefined thresholds to minimize the influence of extreme outliers. This approach maintains a bounded range of values.

Noise Reduction

Smoothing Techniques

- **Moving Average:** Calculates the average of a fixed number of consecutive data points to smooth out short-term fluctuations and highlight longer-term trends.
    - **Simple Moving Average (SMA):** A basic form of moving average that equally weights all data points within the window.
    - **Exponential Moving Average (EMA):** Weighs recent observations more heavily, making it responsive to recent changes.
- **Gaussian Smoothing:** Applies a Gaussian filter to smooth data by averaging with a weighted kernel. It's effective for reducing noise while preserving important features.

Filtering

- **Low-pass Filters:** Remove high-frequency noise while retaining low-frequency components. Suitable for time-series data where high-frequency noise is prevalent.
- **Median Filtering:** Replaces each data point with the median of its neighboring values. It is particularly effective for removing outliers and preserving the edge information in data.

Data Consistency

Standardization and Normalization

- **Standardization:** Transforms data to have a mean of zero and a standard deviation of one. This technique is crucial for algorithms that assume normally distributed data and helps in comparing features on a common scale.
    - **Formula:**

$Z = \frac{(X-\mu)}{\sigma}$, where μ is the mean and σ is the standard deviation.

- **Normalization:** Scales data to a fixed range, typically [0, 1]. This technique is important for algorithms that require data to be within a specific range.

- **Min-Max Scaling Formula:**

$X_{norm} = \frac{(X - X_{min})}{(X_{max} - X_{min})}$, where Xmin and Xmax are the minimum and maximum values of the feature.

Formatting and Integration

- **Unit Conversion:** Ensures that all data is in consistent units (e.g., converting temperature readings from Celsius to Fahrenheit). This step is crucial for accurate analysis and comparison.
- **Data Merging:** Integrates data from multiple sources or sensors into a single dataset. Techniques include:
  - **Joining Data:** Combining datasets using common keys (e.g., timestamps or identifiers) to create a unified dataset.
  - **Concatenation:** Appending datasets along a specific axis (e.g., stacking data vertically or horizontally).

Data Preprocessing Techniques - Feature Engineering

Feature Extraction

- **Creating New Features:** Deriving new features from existing data to enhance model performance. Examples include:
  - **Time-Based Features:** Extracting components like day of the week, hour of the day from timestamp data to capture temporal patterns.
  - **Interaction Features:** Creating features that represent interactions between existing features (e.g., multiplying or combining features).
- **Dimensionality Reduction:** Techniques to reduce the number of features while retaining important information. Common methods include:
  - **Principal Component Analysis (PCA):** Projects data onto a lower-dimensional space by maximizing variance, useful for reducing redundancy and improving model efficiency.
  - **t-Distributed Stochastic Neighbor Embedding (t-SNE):** A technique for visualizing high-dimensional data in lower dimensions, preserving local structure.

Feature Selection

- **Filter Methods:** Select features based on statistical tests or metrics. Common methods include:
    - **Chi-Square Test:** Assesses the independence between categorical features and the target variable.
    - **ANOVA (Analysis of Variance):** Evaluates the variance between groups to determine feature relevance.
- **Wrapper Methods:** Evaluate feature subsets by training and testing models. Techniques include:
    - **Recursive Feature Elimination (RFE):** Iteratively removes the least important features based on model performance.
- **Embedded Methods:** Feature selection integrated into model training. Examples include:
    - **LASSO (Least Absolute Shrinkage and Selection Operator):** Adds a penalty to the regression model based on the absolute value of feature coefficients, promoting sparsity.

Data Transformation

Scaling and Normalization

- **Min-Max Scaling:** Rescales features to a specific range, typically [0, 1]. It ensures that features contribute equally to the analysis.
- **Z-Score Normalization:** Transforms data to have a mean of zero and a standard deviation of one, useful for algorithms assuming normality.

Encoding Categorical Data

- **One-Hot Encoding:** Converts categorical variables into binary vectors, creating separate columns for each category. It's essential for algorithms that require numerical input.
- **Label Encoding:** Assigns unique numerical labels to categorical values, suitable for ordinal data where there is a meaningful order.

Handling Temporal Data

- **Time Series Decomposition:** Breaks down time series data into trend, seasonal, and residual components. Useful for identifying underlying patterns and forecasting.

- **Lag Features:** Creates features representing previous time steps (e.g., lagged values, rolling statistics) to capture temporal dependencies and improve model performance.

Data Augmentation

Synthetic Data Generation

- **Interpolation:** Generates additional data points by interpolating between existing values, enhancing dataset size and model robustness.
- **Simulation:** Creates synthetic data based on theoretical models or simulations to supplement real data and improve analysis.

Data Synthesis

- **Oversampling:** Techniques like Synthetic Minority Over-sampling Technique (SMOTE) generate synthetic samples for underrepresented classes in imbalanced datasets.
- **Undersampling:** Reduces the number of samples in overrepresented classes to balance the dataset and improve model performance.

Practical Considerations

Tools and Technologies

- **Data Cleaning Software:** Tools like OpenRefine, Talend, and Trifacta offer user-friendly interfaces for data cleaning and preprocessing, with features for handling missing data, outliers, and more.
- **Programming Languages:** Python (with libraries such as Pandas, NumPy, and Scikit-learn) and R (with packages like dplyr, tidyr) are widely used for data manipulation and preprocessing.

Best Practices

- **Documenting Processes:** Maintain detailed records of data cleaning and preprocessing steps to ensure reproducibility and facilitate future analyses.
- **Automating Workflows:** Implement automated data cleaning pipelines to handle repetitive tasks and maintain consistency across datasets.

- **Continuous Monitoring:** Regularly monitor data quality and update preprocessing techniques to adapt to changes in data patterns and sources.

Data cleaning and preprocessing are crucial for preparing data for analysis and ensuring the accuracy and reliability of insights derived from it. By employing techniques such as handling missing data, detecting and treating outliers, reducing noise, and transforming features, organizations can improve the quality of their data and enhance the performance of their analytical models. Understanding and applying these techniques effectively is vital for managing complex datasets and achieving successful outcomes in data-driven projects. As data complexity and volume increase, continued advancements in cleaning and preprocessing techniques will play a key role in harnessing the full potential of data.

4. Feature Extraction and Selection for Health Assessment

Feature extraction and selection are crucial processes in data analysis and machine learning, particularly for applications such as health assessment. These techniques help in identifying and leveraging the most relevant features from complex datasets, enhancing the predictive performance of models and providing actionable insights. This detailed overview explores the methodologies and techniques for feature extraction and selection, focusing on their applications in health assessment.

4.1 Identifying Relevant Features for Health Assessment

Importance of Identifying Relevant Features

In health assessment, whether for medical diagnostics or monitoring industrial systems, identifying the most relevant features is crucial. Relevant features are those that provide significant information about the health status or performance of the system being evaluated.

Medical Context

In medical contexts, relevant features might include:

- **Physiological Metrics:** Parameters such as heart rate, blood pressure, blood glucose levels, and cholesterol levels are often monitored to assess health conditions. For instance, elevated blood pressure is a known risk factor for cardiovascular diseases.
- **Diagnostic Test Results:** Features from lab tests, such as blood test results (e.g., hemoglobin levels, liver function tests) and imaging results (e.g., tumor size in MRI scans), are crucial for diagnosing conditions.
- **Clinical Symptoms:** Data on symptoms reported by patients, such as pain levels or frequency of headaches, are used to assess health and predict outcomes.

Industrial Context

For industrial systems like transformers, relevant features include:

- **Temperature:** Monitoring operating temperature helps in identifying potential overheating issues that could lead to failures.
- **Vibration:** Vibration data can reveal mechanical issues, misalignment, or imbalances.
- **Oil Quality:** In transformers, the quality of insulation oil, including moisture levels and breakdown voltage, is crucial for assessing insulation health and potential failures.
- **Electrical Parameters:** Features such as harmonic distortion, load current, and voltage levels are monitored to assess performance and diagnose issues.

Approaches to Identifying Relevant Features

Domain Knowledge

- **Medical Expertise:** Healthcare professionals use their expertise to determine which metrics are most indicative of health conditions. For instance, cardiologists might focus on ECG features that signal arrhythmias.
- **Engineering Expertise:** Engineers utilize their knowledge to select features that indicate the health of machinery. For transformers, this might involve selecting parameters linked to electrical and mechanical health.

Statistical Analysis

- **Correlation Analysis:** Measures the relationship between features and outcomes. Features with high correlation to the target variable (e.g., disease presence) are considered relevant.
  - **Pearson Correlation:** Measures linear relationships between continuous variables.
  - **Spearman Rank Correlation:** Assesses monotonic relationships, suitable for ordinal or non-normally distributed data.
- **Hypothesis Testing:** Statistical tests (e.g., t-tests, ANOVA) evaluate whether features significantly differ between groups, such as patients with and without a condition.

Exploratory Data Analysis (EDA)

- **Visualization Techniques:** Tools like scatter plots, histograms, and heatmaps help visualize the relationships and distributions of features. EDA can reveal patterns and anomalies.
- **Distribution Analysis:** Understanding feature distributions helps in identifying which features have significant variance or skewness.

Domain-Specific Considerations

- **Medical Imaging:** Features from images (e.g., tumor size, shape, texture) are extracted using image processing techniques and are crucial for diagnostic accuracy.
- **Industrial Monitoring:** For transformers, features like harmonic distortion or moisture content are monitored to predict failures and ensure operational efficiency.

4.2 Techniques for Feature Extraction

Feature extraction involves transforming raw data into meaningful features that can be used for modeling. This process depends on the type of data and the specific requirements of the health assessment.

Statistical Methods - Descriptive Statistics

- **Central Tendency Measures:** Mean and median provide insights into the average values and central location of the data.
- **Dispersion Measures:** Variance and standard deviation describe the spread and variability of the features.
- **Skewness and Kurtosis:** These measures assess the asymmetry and peakedness of feature distributions, respectively, providing insights into the shape of the data distribution.

Principal Component Analysis (PCA)

PCA is a widely used technique for dimensionality reduction, transforming data into a new coordinate system where the greatest variances are captured.

- **Standardization:** Data is standardized to have zero mean and unit variance to ensure that all features contribute equally.

- **Covariance Matrix Calculation:** Computes the covariance matrix to understand the relationships between features.
- **Eigenvalue Decomposition:** Finds eigenvalues and eigenvectors of the covariance matrix. Principal components are the eigenvectors corresponding to the largest eigenvalues.
- **Dimensionality Reduction:** Selects principal components that explain the most variance, reducing the feature space while retaining essential information.

Linear Discriminant Analysis (LDA)

LDA is used for both dimensionality reduction and classification, focusing on maximizing the separation between different classes.

- **Scatter Matrices:** Computes within-class and between-class scatter matrices to measure the variance within each class and the variance between classes.
- **Eigenvalue Decomposition:** Finds eigenvalues and eigenvectors that maximize class separability. The new axes (discriminants) are used to project data onto a lower-dimensional space.

Signal Processing Techniques

Fourier Transform

The Fourier Transform decomposes signals into their constituent frequencies, providing insights into the frequency content of time-domain signals.

- **Discrete Fourier Transform (DFT):** Converts discrete time-domain signals into frequency-domain representations.
- **Fast Fourier Transform (FFT):** An efficient algorithm for computing the DFT, enabling real-time frequency analysis.

Wavelet Transform

Wavelet Transform provides a time-frequency representation of signals, capturing both time and frequency information.

- **Continuous Wavelet Transform (CWT):** Offers a continuous decomposition of a signal into wavelets, useful for analyzing non-stationary signals.
- **Discrete Wavelet Transform (DWT):** Decomposes a signal into discrete wavelet coefficients, useful for feature extraction and compression.

Short-Time Fourier Transform (STFT)

STFT analyzes signals in short overlapping windows to provide a time-frequency representation, capturing how frequency content evolves over time.

Filtering Techniques

Filtering techniques help in isolating relevant features from noisy data.

- **Low-Pass Filters:** Allow low-frequency components to pass through while attenuating high-frequency noise.
- **High-Pass Filters:** Remove low-frequency trends and retain high-frequency details.
- **Band-Pass Filters:** Isolate specific frequency ranges, useful for focusing on particular signal characteristics.

Domain-Specific Techniques

Medical Imaging

- **Texture Analysis:** Extracts features related to the texture of medical images, such as homogeneity and entropy, which can be indicative of disease presence.
- **Segmentation:** Identifies and extracts regions of interest from images, such as tumors or organs, for further analysis.
- **Shape Analysis:** Analyzes the shape and structure of features within images to diagnose conditions based on anatomical abnormalities.

Vibration Analysis

- **Spectral Features:** Extracts features from the frequency domain, such as peak frequency, harmonic content, and spectral entropy, to assess mechanical health.

- **Time-Domain Features:** Measures like RMS (Root Mean Square), peak-to-peak, and kurtosis are used to characterize the vibration signal and detect anomalies.

4.3 Feature Selection Algorithms

Feature selection involves choosing a subset of features that contribute most to the model's performance. Effective feature selection helps in improving model accuracy, reducing overfitting, and decreasing computational costs.

Filter Methods

Statistical Tests

- **Chi-Square Test:** Evaluates the independence between categorical features and the target variable. Features with high chi-square scores are considered significant.
- **ANOVA (Analysis of Variance):** Compares means between different groups to identify features that significantly impact the target variable.

Correlation-Based Feature Selection

- **Pearson Correlation:** Measures linear relationships between features and the target. Features with high absolute correlation values are deemed important.
- **Spearman Rank Correlation:** Assesses monotonic relationships and is suitable for non-parametric data.

Wrapper Methods

Recursive Feature Elimination (RFE)

RFE is a wrapper method that iteratively removes the least important features based on model performance.

- **Model Training:** Train a model using all features.
- **Feature Ranking:** Evaluate feature importance using model coefficients or performance metrics.
- **Feature Removal:** Remove the least important features and retrain the model.

- **Iteration:** Repeat until the desired number of features is achieved.

Genetic Algorithms

Genetic algorithms optimize feature subsets by simulating evolutionary processes.

- **Initial Population:** Generate an initial population of feature subsets.
- **Fitness Evaluation:** Assess each subset's performance using a fitness function, such as model accuracy.
- **Selection, Crossover, and Mutation:** Create new subsets through crossover and mutation of selected features.
- **Evolution:** Evolve the population over generations to find the optimal feature subset.

Embedded Methods

LASSO (Least Absolute Shrinkage and Selection Operator)

LASSO performs feature selection during model training by applying an L1 penalty.

- **L1 Regularization:** Adds a penalty proportional to the absolute value of feature coefficients, promoting sparsity and setting less important coefficients to zero.

Ridge Regression

Ridge regression applies an L2 penalty to the loss function, reducing the impact of less important features but not eliminating them.

- **L2 Regularization:** Adds a penalty proportional to the square of feature coefficients, controlling multicollinearity and reducing model complexity.

Decision Trees

Decision trees perform feature selection by evaluating feature importance during the tree-building process.

- **Impurity Reduction:** Features that reduce impurity (e.g., Gini impurity, entropy) are deemed important for splitting nodes in the tree.

Hybrid Methods

Hybrid methods combine filter, wrapper, and embedded approaches to leverage their strengths.

- **Example:** Use a filter method to initially reduce the feature space and then apply wrapper methods to fine-tune feature selection based on model performance.

Applications in Health Assessment

Medical Diagnostics

In medical diagnostics, feature extraction and selection are used to improve the accuracy and efficiency of diagnostic models.

- **Disease Prediction:** Features extracted from medical data (e.g., imaging, lab tests) are used to build predictive models for various diseases. For example, using features from MRI scans to predict tumor malignancy.
- **Patient Monitoring:** Continuous monitoring of physiological metrics (e.g., heart rate, blood pressure) involves feature extraction techniques to track changes over time and detect anomalies.

Industrial Health Monitoring

For industrial systems like transformers, feature extraction and selection help in monitoring and predicting equipment health.

- **Failure Prediction:** Features such as temperature and vibration patterns are used to predict potential failures. For example, extracting features from vibration data to detect misalignments or imbalances.
- **Maintenance Scheduling:** By analyzing features related to equipment performance, maintenance schedules can be optimized to prevent unexpected breakdowns.

Future Directions

Advances in Machine Learning

Machine learning techniques, including deep learning, offer new opportunities for feature extraction and selection.

- **Automated Feature Engineering:** Advanced algorithms can automate feature extraction from raw data, reducing the need for manual feature engineering.
- **Deep Learning:** Neural networks can automatically learn complex features from data, particularly in domains like medical imaging.

Integration with Big Data

The integration of feature extraction and selection techniques with big data technologies enables the handling of large-scale datasets, leading to more accurate and scalable health assessment models.

- **Real-Time Analysis:** Advanced techniques and computing power facilitate real-time feature extraction and analysis, improving timely decision-making in health monitoring.

Personalized Health Assessment

Personalized health assessment involves tailoring feature extraction and selection to individual patients, enhancing the accuracy of predictions and diagnoses.

- **Customized Models:** Features can be customized based on individual health profiles, improving the relevance and effectiveness of health assessments.

Feature extraction and selection are fundamental processes in health assessment, crucial for transforming raw data into meaningful insights. Through statistical methods, signal processing techniques, and domain-specific approaches, relevant features are identified and processed to enhance model performance. Techniques such as PCA, LDA, and various feature selection algorithms ensure that models are accurate, efficient, and interpretable.

In medical diagnostics and industrial health monitoring, these techniques play a vital role in improving predictive accuracy, optimizing maintenance schedules, and personalizing health assessments. As technology evolves, advancements in machine learning and big data will continue to shape the future of feature extraction and selection, leading to more effective and personalized health assessment solutions.

5. Predictive Maintenance Models: A Comprehensive Overview

Predictive maintenance (PdM) is an advanced strategy that leverages data-driven insights to forecast equipment failures before they occur. By employing various predictive techniques and machine learning models, organizations can optimize maintenance schedules, reduce downtime, and improve overall operational efficiency. This extensive overview covers predictive maintenance concepts, machine learning models applicable to predictive maintenance, and case studies focusing on predictive maintenance in transformers.

5.1 Overview of Predictive Maintenance Concepts

Definition and Objectives

Predictive maintenance involves monitoring the condition of equipment through various sensors and data analytics to predict when maintenance should be performed. The primary objectives are to:

- **Prevent Unplanned Downtime:** By forecasting failures, organizations can perform maintenance before breakdowns occur, reducing unexpected downtimes.
- **Optimize Maintenance Schedules:** Shift from time-based maintenance schedules to condition-based schedules, improving resource utilization.
- **Extend Equipment Life:** Regular and timely maintenance can extend the operational life of equipment.
- **Reduce Maintenance Costs:** Preventive actions are typically less costly than emergency repairs or replacements.

Predictive Maintenance vs. Other Maintenance Strategies

- **Reactive Maintenance:** Maintenance is performed only after equipment fails. It often leads to higher downtime and repair costs.
- **Preventive Maintenance:** Scheduled maintenance based on time intervals or usage, which may not always align with actual equipment condition.

- **Condition-Based Maintenance:** Maintenance performed when certain indicators suggest that equipment is failing or is about to fail. Predictive maintenance takes this a step further by using data analytics to foresee potential failures before they happen.

Data Sources and Types

Effective predictive maintenance relies on various data sources:

- **Sensor Data:** Continuous monitoring of parameters like temperature, vibration, pressure, and humidity.
- **Operational Data:** Information on equipment usage, load, and operating conditions.
- **Historical Maintenance Records:** Data on past failures, repairs, and maintenance activities.
- **Environmental Data:** External factors such as ambient temperature and humidity that may affect equipment performance.

Data Acquisition Methods

- **Sensors and IoT Devices:** Sensors embedded in equipment collect real-time data. Internet of Things (IoT) devices enable the integration of sensor data with cloud-based analytics.
- **Manual Data Entry:** Historical data and operational logs that are manually recorded and entered into databases.
- **Automated Data Collection Systems:** Systems that automatically gather and store data from various sources.

Challenges in Predictive Maintenance

- **Data Quality and Integrity:** Ensuring data accuracy and completeness is crucial for reliable predictions.
- **Data Integration:** Combining data from different sources can be complex and requires robust data management systems.
- **Algorithm Selection:** Choosing the right predictive model and tuning it for specific equipment and conditions.
- **Scalability:** Implementing predictive maintenance solutions across multiple assets and locations can be challenging.

5.2 Machine Learning Models for Predictive Maintenance

Machine learning (ML) models play a critical role in predictive maintenance by analyzing historical and real-time data to forecast equipment failures. These models can be categorized into regression and classification models, each with specific applications and methodologies.

Regression Models

Regression models predict continuous outcomes, such as the remaining useful life (RUL) of equipment or the time until failure.

Linear Regression

- **Overview:** Linear regression models the relationship between a dependent variable (e.g., failure time) and one or more independent variables (e.g., sensor readings).
- **Application:** Useful for straightforward relationships and can provide insights into how specific features affect failure times.
- **Limitations:** May not capture complex, non-linear relationships or interactions between features.

Polynomial Regression

- **Overview:** Extends linear regression by adding polynomial terms to capture non-linear relationships between variables.
- **Application:** Useful when data shows non-linear trends that cannot be captured by linear models.
- **Limitations:** Can lead to overfitting if the polynomial degree is too high.

Support Vector Regression (SVR)

- **Overview:** SVR is a type of support vector machine that handles regression tasks by finding a function that deviates from the actual data by at most a specified margin.
- **Application:** Effective in capturing non-linear relationships with a robust performance against outliers.
- **Limitations:** Can be computationally intensive and require careful parameter tuning.

Decision Tree Regression

- **Overview:** Uses decision tree algorithms to model data by dividing it into subsets based on feature values, predicting continuous outcomes at the leaves of the tree.
- **Application:** Handles complex relationships and interactions between features well.
- **Limitations:** Prone to overfitting, especially with deep trees.

Ensemble Methods

- **Random Forest Regression:** Combines multiple decision trees to improve prediction accuracy and robustness.
- **Gradient Boosting Machines (GBM):** Builds models iteratively to correct errors made by previous models, enhancing predictive performance.

Classification Models

Classification models predict discrete outcomes, such as whether equipment will fail within a certain time frame.

Logistic Regression

- **Overview:** Models the probability of a binary outcome based on one or more predictor variables.
- **Application:** Useful for predicting the likelihood of failure (e.g., failure vs. non-failure).
- **Limitations:** Assumes a linear relationship between predictors and the log odds of the outcome.

Decision Trees

- **Overview:** Classifies data by splitting it into subsets based on feature values, leading to a decision tree structure with nodes representing features and leaves representing outcomes.
- **Application:** Useful for capturing complex, non-linear relationships and interactions.
- **Limitations:** Can be prone to overfitting, especially with deep trees.

Random Forest Classification

- **Overview:** An ensemble method that combines multiple decision trees to improve classification accuracy and generalizability.

- **Application:** Provides better performance and robustness compared to individual decision trees.
- **Limitations:** Can be computationally intensive and less interpretable.

Support Vector Machines (SVM)

- **Overview:** Classifies data by finding a hyperplane that maximizes the margin between different classes.
- **Application:** Effective for high-dimensional data and complex decision boundaries.
- **Limitations:** Requires careful parameter tuning and can be computationally demanding.

Neural Networks

- **Overview:** Composed of interconnected nodes (neurons) organized in layers, neural networks can model complex, non-linear relationships.
- **Application:** Useful for handling large-scale data and capturing intricate patterns.
- **Limitations:** Requires significant computational resources and data for training.

Ensemble Classification

- **Gradient Boosting Classifiers:** Builds models iteratively to correct errors from previous classifiers, enhancing classification performance.
- **Voting Classifiers:** Combines predictions from multiple classifiers to improve accuracy and robustness.

Model Evaluation and Validation

Evaluating and validating predictive maintenance models is crucial to ensure their reliability and performance.

Metrics for Regression Models

- **Mean Absolute Error (MAE):** Measures the average absolute difference between predicted and actual values.
- **Mean Squared Error (MSE):** Measures the average squared difference between predicted and actual values.

- **Root Mean Squared Error (RMSE):** The square root of MSE, providing an error metric in the same unit as the target variable.
- **R-Squared (R^2):** Indicates the proportion of variance explained by the model.

Metrics for Classification Models

- **Accuracy:** The proportion of correctly classified instances over the total number of instances.
- **Precision:** The proportion of true positive predictions among all positive predictions.
- **Recall (Sensitivity):** The proportion of true positive predictions among all actual positives.
- **F1 Score:** The harmonic mean of precision and recall, providing a balanced measure of performance.
- **Receiver Operating Characteristic (ROC) Curve:** A graphical representation of the trade-off between true positive rate and false positive rate.

Cross-Validation

- **K-Fold Cross-Validation:** Divides the data into K subsets and performs training and validation K times, ensuring each subset is used for validation once.
- **Leave-One-Out Cross-Validation (LOOCV):** A special case of K-fold cross-validation where K equals the number of data points.

5.3 Case Studies of Predictive Maintenance in Transformers

Transformers are critical components in electrical power systems, and their reliable operation is essential for maintaining grid stability and efficiency. Predictive maintenance for transformers involves monitoring various parameters and applying predictive models to foresee potential issues. Here are detailed case studies showcasing the application of predictive maintenance in transformers.

Case Study 1: Predictive Maintenance for Transformer Overheating

Background

Overheating in transformers can lead to insulation degradation, reduced efficiency, and ultimately, failure. Predictive maintenance can help in identifying overheating conditions before they lead to serious problems.

Data Collection

- **Parameters Monitored:** Transformer temperature, load levels, cooling system status, and ambient temperature.
- **Sensors Used:** Temperature sensors, load sensors, and cooling system sensors.

Feature Extraction

- **Temperature Trends:** Extract features related to temperature trends over time.
- **Load Patterns:** Analyze load patterns and their impact on temperature.
- **Cooling Efficiency:** Measure cooling system performance and its effect on transformer temperature.

Predictive Models

- **Regression Analysis:** Used to model the relationship between temperature, load, and failure time. Polynomial regression helps in capturing non-linear relationships between variables.
- **Support Vector Regression (SVR):** Applied to predict the time until overheating occurs based on historical temperature and load data.
- **Random Forest Regression:** Used to improve prediction accuracy by combining multiple decision trees.

Results and Benefits

- **Accuracy Improvement:** The predictive models significantly improved the accuracy of failure time predictions.
- **Reduced Downtime:** Early detection of overheating issues allowed for timely maintenance, reducing transformer downtime.
- **Extended Equipment Life:** Regular maintenance based on predictive insights helped in extending the operational life of transformers.

Case Study 2: Vibration Analysis for Transformer Fault Detection

Background

Vibration analysis is critical for detecting mechanical faults in transformers, such as misalignment or imbalance. Predictive maintenance can identify these issues before they lead to equipment failure.

Data Collection

- **Parameters Monitored:** Vibration levels, frequency spectra, and vibration patterns.
- **Sensors Used:** Vibration sensors and accelerometers.

Feature Extraction

- **Spectral Features:** Extract features from frequency spectra, including peak frequencies and harmonic content.
- **Time-Domain Features:** Analyze features such as RMS (Root Mean Square) and kurtosis to identify anomalies.
- **Wavelet Features:** Use wavelet transforms to capture time-frequency characteristics of vibration signals.

Predictive Models

- **Classification Models:** Logistic regression and decision trees used to classify vibration patterns as normal or faulty.
- **Ensemble Methods:** Random Forest and Gradient Boosting applied to improve classification performance.
- **Neural Networks:** Deep learning models used to capture complex patterns in vibration data and predict potential faults.

Results and Benefits

- **Early Fault Detection:** Predictive models identified faults in their early stages, preventing major failures.

- **Improved Maintenance Planning:** Maintenance activities were scheduled based on predictive insights, optimizing resource allocation.
- **Cost Savings:** Reduced emergency repairs and extended transformer life resulted in significant cost savings.

Case Study 3: Oil Quality Monitoring for Transformer Health

Background

The quality of transformer oil is crucial for insulation performance and overall transformer health. Predictive maintenance can help in assessing oil quality and predicting potential failures.

Data Collection

- **Parameters Monitored:** Moisture content, dielectric strength, and dissolved gas levels.
- **Sensors Used:** Oil quality sensors and gas chromatography devices.

Feature Extraction

- **Moisture Content Trends:** Extract features related to moisture content changes over time.
- **Dielectric Strength:** Analyze the dielectric strength of oil to assess insulation performance.
- **Dissolved Gas Analysis:** Use gas chromatography data to identify the presence of gases indicative of potential faults.

Predictive Models

- **Regression Models:** Linear and polynomial regression used to predict oil degradation and its impact on transformer health.
- **Support Vector Machines (SVM):** Applied to classify oil quality into different health categories.
- **Ensemble Methods:** Random Forest and Gradient Boosting used to enhance predictive accuracy.

Results and Benefits

- **Improved Diagnostics:** Predictive models provided accurate assessments of oil quality and transformer health.
- **Timely Maintenance:** Maintenance activities were performed based on oil quality predictions, preventing potential failures.
- **Enhanced Reliability:** Regular monitoring and timely maintenance improved transformer reliability and performance.

Future Directions and Innovations

Advances in Machine Learning and AI

- **Deep Learning:** Utilization of advanced neural networks for feature extraction and prediction, capable of handling large-scale and complex data.
- **Explainable AI:** Development of models that provide interpretable results, enhancing understanding and trust in predictive maintenance outcomes.

Integration with IoT and Big Data

- **Real-Time Monitoring:** Integration of IoT devices for real-time data collection and analysis, improving the accuracy of predictive maintenance models.
- **Big Data Analytics:** Leveraging big data technologies to handle and analyze large volumes of data from multiple sources.

Personalized Predictive Maintenance

- **Customized Models:** Development of predictive models tailored to specific equipment and operating conditions, improving accuracy and effectiveness.
- **Adaptive Maintenance Schedules:** Dynamic adjustment of maintenance schedules based on real-time data and predictive insights.

Enhanced Data Integration and Management

- **Unified Data Platforms:** Creation of integrated data platforms that consolidate data from various sources, facilitating comprehensive analysis and insights.

- **Data Quality Improvement:** Focus on ensuring data accuracy and integrity for reliable predictive maintenance outcomes.

Predictive maintenance represents a significant advancement over traditional maintenance strategies, offering the potential to optimize equipment performance, reduce downtime, and lower maintenance costs. By leveraging machine learning models, organizations can effectively analyze complex data to predict equipment failures and schedule timely maintenance.

This detailed overview has explored the core concepts of predictive maintenance, various machine learning models used in this domain, and case studies demonstrating their application in transformers. As technology evolves, advancements in machine learning, big data, and IoT will continue to drive innovation in predictive maintenance, leading to more accurate, efficient, and personalized solutions.

6. Anomaly Detection in Predictive Maintenance: Techniques and Applications

Anomaly detection is a crucial component of predictive maintenance, particularly in monitoring complex systems such as transformers. By identifying unusual patterns or deviations from normal operation, anomaly detection helps in predicting equipment failures, ensuring timely maintenance, and improving overall reliability. This detailed overview explores various anomaly detection techniques, the application of AI models in detecting anomalies in transformer data, and provides illustrative case studies.

6.1 Techniques for Anomaly Detection

Anomaly detection methods can be broadly categorized into statistical, machine learning-based, and hybrid techniques. Each method has its strengths and is chosen based on the nature of the data and the specific requirements of the maintenance strategy.

Statistical Techniques

Statistical Techniques rely on mathematical models to identify deviations from expected patterns or distributions.

- **Z-Score Analysis:**
  - **Overview:** Measures the number of standard deviations a data point is from the mean of a distribution. A high Z-score indicates an anomaly.
  - **Application:** Useful for detecting outliers in normally distributed data.
  - **Limitations:** Assumes data follows a Gaussian distribution, which might not always be the case.
- **Moving Average Control Charts:**
  - **Overview:** Uses moving averages and control limits to monitor data trends over time. Data points falling outside control limits are flagged as anomalies.
  - **Application:** Effective for detecting shifts or trends in time-series data.

  - **Limitations:** May not handle complex or multi-dimensional data well.
- **Exponential Smoothing:**
  - **Overview:** A technique that applies weighted averages of past observations with an exponentially decreasing weight. Anomalies are detected when actual values deviate significantly from smoothed values.
  - **Application:** Suitable for time-series data with a trend or seasonality.
  - **Limitations:** Performance depends on the choice of smoothing parameters.

Machine Learning-Based Techniques

Machine Learning-Based Techniques leverage algorithms to identify anomalies based on learned patterns from data.

- **Clustering-Based Techniques:**
  - **K-Means Clustering:**
    - **Overview:** Partitions data into K clusters based on feature similarity. Points that do not fit well into any cluster are considered anomalies.
    - **Application:** Useful when the number of clusters is known and data is well-separated.
    - **Limitations:** Assumes clusters are spherical and equally sized.
  - **DBSCAN (Density-Based Spatial Clustering of Applications with Noise):**
    - **Overview:** Identifies clusters based on density, labeling points that lie in low-density regions as anomalies.
    - **Application:** Effective for detecting clusters of varying shapes and sizes.
    - **Limitations:** Performance depends on parameter choices and may struggle with varying densities.
- **Outlier Detection Techniques:**
  - **Isolation Forest:**
    - **Overview:** Builds random trees to isolate data points. Points that are isolated quickly are considered anomalies.
    - **Application:** Scales well with high-dimensional data and large datasets.
    - **Limitations:** Requires tuning of parameters for optimal performance.

- **Local Outlier Factor (LOF):**
  - **Overview:** Measures the local density deviation of a data point compared to its neighbors. Points with significantly lower densities are flagged as anomalies.
  - **Application:** Effective for detecting anomalies in multi-dimensional data.
  - **Limitations:** Sensitive to the choice of parameters and the number of neighbors.
- **One-Class SVM (Support Vector Machine):**
  - **Overview:** Trains on normal data to learn a decision boundary that separates normal instances from anomalies.
  - **Application:** Suitable for cases where anomalies are rare and normal data is abundant.
  - **Limitations:** Computationally intensive and sensitive to parameter choices.

- **Neural Network-Based Techniques:**
  - **Autoencoders:**
    - **Overview:** Neural networks designed to learn a compressed representation of data. Anomalies are detected based on reconstruction errors, with high errors indicating anomalies.
    - **Application:** Effective for complex, high dimensional data.
    - **Limitations:** Requires large amounts of data and tuning of network architecture.
  - **Variational Autoencoders (VAEs):**
    - **Overview:** A probabilistic variant of autoencoders that models data distributions. Anomalies are detected based on deviations from learned distributions.
    - **Application:** Suitable for handling uncertainty and generating new data samples.
    - **Limitations:** More complex and computationally demanding compared to traditional autoencoders.

Hybrid Techniques

Hybrid Techniques combine multiple methods to improve anomaly detection performance.

- **Combining Clustering and Outlier Detection:**
  - **Overview:** Use clustering to identify potential anomalies and then apply outlier detection techniques to refine results.
  - **Application:** Enhances detection capabilities by leveraging the strengths of different methods.

  - **Limitations:** Complexity increases with the combination of methods.
- **Integrating Machine Learning with Statistical Techniques:**
  - **Overview:** Use statistical methods to pre-process data and machine learning algorithms for final anomaly detection.
  - **Application:** Provides a balanced approach to handle different data characteristics.
  - **Limitations:** Requires careful design to ensure the integration improves overall performance.

6.2 Application of AI Models for Detecting Anomalies in Transformer Data

Transformers are critical components in electrical power systems, and their maintenance is essential for ensuring reliable operation. AI models play a significant role in detecting anomalies in transformer data by analyzing various parameters and identifying patterns that indicate potential issues.

AI Models for Transformer Anomaly Detection

- **Sensor Data Analysis:**
  - **Temperature Sensors:** Monitor transformer temperature to detect overheating issues. AI models analyze temperature trends to predict potential failures.
  - **Vibration Sensors:** Track vibrations to identify mechanical faults such as misalignment or imbalance. Machine learning models classify vibration patterns to detect anomalies.
  - **Oil Quality Sensors:** Measure parameters like moisture content and dielectric strength. AI models predict oil degradation and assess transformer health based on oil quality.
- **Machine Learning Models:**
  - **Autoencoders:** Used for detecting anomalies in temperature, vibration, and oil quality data. Autoencoders learn normal operating patterns and detect deviations as anomalies.
  - **Isolation Forest:** Applied to high-dimensional sensor data to identify outliers. Effective in large datasets where traditional methods may fail.
  - **Local Outlier Factor (LOF):** Analyzes local densities in sensor data to detect anomalies. Useful for identifying unusual patterns in complex data.

AI-Driven Anomaly Detection Workflow

1. **Data Collection:** Continuous monitoring of transformer parameters using various sensors.
2. **Pre-Processing:** Cleaning and normalizing data to ensure consistency and accuracy.

3. **Feature Extraction:** Identifying relevant features from raw data, such as trends, patterns, and statistical measures.
4. **Model Training:** Training AI models using historical data to learn normal operating patterns.
5. **Anomaly Detection:** Applying trained models to real-time data to identify deviations from expected patterns.
6. **Alert Generation:** Generating alerts for maintenance teams when anomalies are detected.
7. **Analysis and Action:** Analyzing detected anomalies to determine the cause and schedule maintenance if needed.

6.3 Examples and Case Studies

Case Study 1: Temperature Anomaly Detection

- **Background:** Transformer overheating can lead to insulation degradation and failure. Anomaly detection in temperature data helps prevent such issues.
- **Data Collection:** Monitored temperature readings from transformers using temperature sensors.
- **Model Used:** Autoencoders for anomaly detection. The autoencoder was trained on normal temperature data to learn typical temperature patterns.
- **Results:** The model successfully identified temperature anomalies that were indicative of overheating conditions. Maintenance teams were alerted to inspect and address the issues before major failures occurred.

Case Study 2: Vibration Analysis for Mechanical Faults

- **Background:** Mechanical faults in transformers, such as misalignment or imbalance, can cause vibrations. Anomaly detection helps in early identification of such faults.
- **Data Collection:** Collected vibration data from accelerometers installed on transformers.
- **Model Used:** Isolation Forest and Local Outlier Factor (LOF). The Isolation Forest identified potential outliers in vibration data, while LOF refined the results by analyzing local density deviations.
- **Results:** The combined approach improved the detection of mechanical faults, leading to timely maintenance actions and reduced transformer downtime.

Case Study 3: Oil Quality Monitoring

- **Background:** Transformer oil quality is crucial for insulation performance. Predicting oil degradation helps in maintaining transformer health.
- **Data Collection:** Monitored oil quality parameters such as moisture content and dielectric strength.
- **Model Used:** Variational Autoencoders (VAEs) for detecting anomalies in oil quality data. VAEs modeled the distribution of normal oil quality parameters and identified deviations as anomalies.
- **Results:** The model accurately predicted oil degradation, allowing for timely maintenance and improved transformer reliability.

Anomaly detection is vital for predictive maintenance, especially in complex systems like transformers. By utilizing various techniques, including statistical methods, machine learning models, and hybrid approaches, organizations can effectively identify deviations from normal operation and prevent potential failures.

AI models such as autoencoders, isolation forests, and local outlier factors offer advanced capabilities for detecting anomalies in transformer data. Through continuous monitoring and data analysis, these models enable proactive maintenance, reducing downtime and extending equipment life.

The case studies provided illustrate the practical applications of anomaly detection techniques in real-world scenarios, showcasing their effectiveness in improving transformer reliability and performance.

As technology advances, the integration of AI with predictive maintenance will continue to evolve, offering even more accurate, efficient, and adaptive solutions for anomaly detection and overall equipment management.

7. Health Index and Condition Monitoring

Transformers are crucial components in electrical power systems, and their reliable operation is essential for maintaining grid stability and efficiency. Monitoring the health of transformers through health indices and advanced condition monitoring techniques helps in predicting potential failures, optimizing maintenance schedules, and ensuring operational reliability. This extensive overview delves into the development of health indices for transformers, AI-based methods for condition monitoring, and the integration of health indices into maintenance strategies.

7.1 Development of Health Indices for Transformers

Health indices provide a quantitative measure of the condition of equipment, reflecting its operational health and potential risk of failure. Developing an effective health index involves identifying critical parameters, quantifying their impact, and aggregating them into a single composite score.

Key Parameters for Health Indices

Transformers are monitored using various parameters, each reflecting different aspects of their condition:

- **Temperature:** The operating temperature of key components like windings and insulation. Excessive temperature can indicate potential issues such as overloads or cooling system failures.
- **Vibration:** Vibrations can reveal mechanical issues such as misalignment or imbalance. Monitoring vibration helps in detecting early signs of mechanical faults.
- **Oil Quality:** Transformer oil provides insulation and cooling. Parameters like moisture content, dielectric strength, and dissolved gas levels are critical for assessing oil quality and overall transformer health.
- **Load:** The electrical load on the transformer. Overloading can lead to excessive heating and reduced lifespan.

- **Insulation Resistance:** Measures the resistance of the insulation system. Low insulation resistance can indicate deterioration or faults.

Calculating Health Indices

Individual Parameter Indices

- **Temperature Index:**
  - **Overview:** Based on the temperature readings of key components.
  - **Calculation:** Normalize temperature readings using historical data or manufacturer specifications. Define thresholds for normal, warning, and critical conditions.
- **Vibration Index:**
  - **Overview:** Derived from vibration data and analyzed for patterns.
  - **Calculation:** Use statistical measures (e.g., RMS, peak-to-peak values) and compare against predefined thresholds. Implement frequency domain analysis for more detailed insights.
- **Oil Quality Index:**
  - **Overview:** Reflects the condition of transformer oil based on multiple parameters.
  - **Calculation:** Combine metrics like moisture content and dielectric strength into a composite index. Use weighted averages to reflect the relative importance of each parameter.
- **Insulation Resistance Index:**
  - **Overview:** Measures the insulation's effectiveness.
  - **Calculation:** Track insulation resistance over time and compare to acceptable ranges. Low resistance values can be flagged as potential issues.

Composite Health Index

A composite health index aggregates multiple individual indices into a single score, providing a comprehensive view of the transformer's overall condition:

- **Data Aggregation:**
  - **Normalization:** Standardize individual indices to a common scale to ensure comparability.

  - **Weighting:** Assign weights based on the criticality of each parameter. For example, oil quality might be weighted more heavily due to its importance in insulation and cooling.
- **Index Calculation:**
  - **Weighted Sum:** Calculate the composite index as a weighted sum of individual indices.
  - **Normalization:** Scale the composite index to a predefined range (e.g., 0 to 100) for easy interpretation.
- **Thresholds and Categories:**
  - **Define Thresholds:** Establish thresholds for different health categories (e.g., Excellent, Good, Fair, Poor).
  - **Categorization:** Use the composite index to classify the transformer's health status and determine appropriate actions.

Example of Health Index Calculation

Data Collection

- Temperature readings: 75°C
- Vibration RMS: 0.5 mm/s
- Moisture Content: 0.2%
- Dielectric Strength: 60 kV

Individual Indices

- Temperature Index: Calculated based on historical data and temperature thresholds.
- Vibration Index: Derived from RMS values compared to standard limits.
- Oil Quality Index: Composite of moisture content and dielectric strength with appropriate weighting.

Composite Health Index

- Normalize individual indices to a 0-100 scale.
- Apply weights to each index based on its importance.
- Calculate the weighted sum to obtain the composite health index.

7.2 AI-Based Methods for Condition Monitoring

Artificial Intelligence (AI) and machine learning techniques enhance condition monitoring by providing advanced capabilities for analyzing complex data and predicting potential failures.

Data Collection and Pre-Processing

Data Collection

- **Sensors:** Deploy sensors to continuously monitor parameters such as temperature, vibration, oil quality, and load.
- **Data Integration:** Aggregate data from multiple sources, including sensor readings, historical maintenance records, and operational data.

Data Pre-Processing

- **Cleaning:** Remove noise and errors from raw data to ensure accuracy.
- **Normalization:** Standardize data to a common scale for consistent analysis.
- **Feature Extraction:** Identify and extract relevant features from raw data, such as trends and patterns.

AI Models for Condition Monitoring

Supervised Learning Models

- **Regression Models:**
    - **Linear Regression:** Predicts continuous outcomes such as the remaining useful life (RUL) based on historical data and current conditions.
    - **Polynomial Regression:** Captures non-linear relationships in data, useful for complex patterns in transformer condition.
- **Classification Models:**
    - **Logistic Regression:** Predicts binary outcomes, such as whether a transformer is in a healthy or faulty state.
    - **Decision Trees:** Classify data into different categories based on feature values, providing interpretable results.

Unsupervised Learning Models

- **Clustering Models:**
  - **K-Means Clustering:** Groups data into clusters based on feature similarity, identifying patterns and outliers.
  - **DBSCAN:** Detects clusters of varying shapes and sizes, flagging points in low-density regions as anomalies.
- **Anomaly Detection Models:**
  - **Isolation Forest:** Isolates anomalies by building random trees, effective for high-dimensional data.
  - **Local Outlier Factor (LOF):** Detects anomalies based on local density deviations compared to neighbors.

Deep Learning Models

- **Autoencoders:**
  - **Overview:** Neural networks that learn a compressed representation of data. Anomalies are detected based on reconstruction errors.
  - **Application:** Effective for complex, high-dimensional data.
- **Convolutional Neural Networks (CNNs):**
  - **Overview:** Deep learning models that extract features from data using convolutional layers.
  - **Application:** Useful for analyzing spatial patterns in data, such as vibration signals.
- **Recurrent Neural Networks (RNNs):**
  - **Overview:** Deep learning models designed for sequential data analysis.
  - **Application:** Suitable for time-series data, predicting future states based on historical trends.

AI-Based Monitoring Workflow

1. **Data Collection:** Continuously gather data from sensors and other sources.
2. **Data Pre-Processing:** Clean, normalize, and extract features from raw data.
3. **Model Training:** Train AI models using historical data to learn normal operating patterns and detect anomalies.

4. **Real-Time Monitoring:** Apply trained models to real-time data to identify potential issues.
5. **Alert Generation:** Generate alerts based on model predictions, indicating the need for maintenance or further investigation.
6. **Analysis and Action:** Analyze detected anomalies to determine the cause and take appropriate actions.

7.3 Integration of Health Indices into Maintenance Strategies

Integrating health indices into maintenance strategies enhances decision-making by providing a quantitative measure of equipment condition. This integration helps optimize maintenance schedules, improve resource allocation, and reduce operational costs.

Maintenance Strategies Based on Health Indices

Condition-Based Maintenance (CBM)

- **Overview:** Maintenance actions are triggered based on the condition of equipment, as indicated by health indices.
- **Implementation:** Monitor health indices continuously and perform maintenance when indices fall below predefined thresholds.
- **Benefits:** Reduces unnecessary maintenance activities and focuses resources on equipment that requires attention.

Predictive Maintenance (PdM)

- **Overview:** Uses health indices and predictive models to forecast potential failures and schedule maintenance proactively.
- **Implementation:** Combine health indices with AI-based predictions to estimate the remaining useful life (RUL) and schedule maintenance before failures occur.
- **Benefits:** Minimizes downtime and extends equipment life by addressing issues before they lead to failures.

Preventive Maintenance (PM)

- **Overview:** Scheduled maintenance based on time intervals or usage, complemented by health indices for prioritization.
- **Implementation:** Schedule regular maintenance activities and use health indices to prioritize tasks based on the current condition of equipment.
- **Benefits:** Ensures regular maintenance while focusing on equipment with higher health risks.

Benefits of Integrating Health Indices

- **Improved Decision-Making:** Provides a quantitative basis for maintenance decisions, enhancing the accuracy of scheduling and resource allocation.
- **Optimized Maintenance Schedules:** Adjusts maintenance activities based on the actual condition of equipment, reducing unnecessary interventions.
- **Enhanced Reliability:** Proactively addresses potential issues, improving the overall reliability and performance of transformers.
- **Cost Savings:** Reduces maintenance costs by focusing on critical issues and minimizing unexpected failures and downtime.

Challenges and Considerations

- **Data Quality:** Ensuring accurate and reliable data for calculating health indices is crucial. Poor data quality can lead to incorrect health assessments.
- **Model Complexity:** AI-based models can be complex and require significant computational resources. Balancing model accuracy with computational efficiency is essential.
- **Threshold Selection:** Defining appropriate thresholds for health indices requires careful consideration of equipment specifications and operating conditions.
- **Integration with Existing Systems:** Incorporating health indices into existing maintenance management systems requires seamless integration and data compatibility.

Health indices and condition monitoring are vital components of effective transformer maintenance strategies. By developing comprehensive health indices, leveraging AI-based condition monitoring methods, and integrating these indices into maintenance strategies, organizations can significantly enhance their ability to predict and prevent transformer failures.

Health Index Development: Involves identifying key parameters, calculating individual and composite indices, and defining thresholds for different health categories. This provides a quantitative measure of transformer health and supports informed decision-making.

AI-Based Condition Monitoring: Utilizes advanced machine learning and deep learning techniques to analyze complex data, detect anomalies, and predict potential failures. AI models enhance the accuracy and efficiency of condition monitoring, enabling proactive maintenance.

Integration into Maintenance Strategies: Health indices and AI-based monitoring are integrated into maintenance strategies such as condition-based, predictive, and preventive maintenance. This integration improves decision-making, optimizes maintenance schedules, and enhances transformer reliability.

As technology continues to evolve, the integration of advanced AI techniques and comprehensive health indices will further enhance the effectiveness of transformer condition monitoring and maintenance strategies, ensuring reliable and efficient operation of critical electrical infrastructure.

8. Advanced AI Techniques in Condition Monitoring and Maintenance

In the realm of condition monitoring and maintenance, advanced AI techniques have transformed how data is analyzed and decisions are made. By leveraging deep learning approaches, time-series analysis, and hybrid models, organizations can enhance their predictive capabilities, optimize maintenance strategies, and improve overall operational efficiency. This comprehensive overview delves into various advanced AI techniques, including deep learning models, time-series analysis with AI, and hybrid models combining different AI techniques, providing a detailed explanation of each approach.

8.1 Deep Learning Approaches

Deep learning approaches are pivotal in modern AI for condition monitoring and predictive maintenance due to their ability to model complex relationships in large datasets. Here's a detailed exploration:

Neural Networks

Overview

Neural networks are the backbone of deep learning. They consist of interconnected nodes (neurons) organized in layers, where each layer performs specific functions:

- **Input Layer:** The first layer receives the raw data, such as sensor readings or historical records. Each node in this layer represents a feature or a data point.
- **Hidden Layers:** Intermediate layers where computations are performed. Each neuron in these layers applies an activation function to the weighted sum of inputs to produce outputs. The number and size of hidden layers affect the network's capacity to learn complex patterns.
- **Output Layer:** The final layer that produces the output, such as classification labels (faulty or not) or regression results (predicted time to failure).

Training Neural Networks

Training neural networks involves several steps:

- **Forward Propagation:** Input data is fed into the network, and predictions are generated by passing data through each layer.
- **Loss Function:** The loss function measures how far the network's predictions are from the actual values. Common loss functions include Mean Squared Error for regression and Cross-Entropy Loss for classification.
- **Backpropagation:** This algorithm calculates the gradient of the loss function with respect to each weight by applying the chain rule, propagates these gradients backward through the network, and updates the weights to minimize the loss using optimization algorithms like Gradient Descent.

Applications in Condition Monitoring

- **Fault Detection:** Neural networks can learn intricate patterns and correlations within sensor data, allowing them to identify anomalies that indicate potential equipment faults. For instance, they can detect deviations in vibration patterns that suggest mechanical issues.
- **Health Prediction:** By analyzing historical and real-time data, neural networks can predict the remaining useful life (RUL) of equipment. This helps in scheduling maintenance before equipment failure occurs, thus reducing unplanned downtime.

Convolutional Neural Networks (CNNs)

Overview

CNNs are specifically designed to process grid-like data such as images and time-series data. They excel in automatically learning spatial hierarchies of features:

- **Convolutional Layers:** Apply convolutional filters to detect various features like edges, textures, or patterns in the data. Each filter scans the input data and produces feature maps that highlight specific attributes.

- **Pooling Layers:** Reduce the spatial dimensions of feature maps while retaining essential information. Common pooling operations include Max Pooling (which retains the maximum value from a feature map region) and Average Pooling (which calculates the average value).
- **Fully Connected Layers:** Combine features from convolutional and pooling layers to perform the final classification or regression. These layers operate like traditional neural network layers but work on the aggregated features.

Training CNNs

Training CNNs involves forward propagation and backpropagation similar to traditional neural networks. Additional techniques include:

- **Data Augmentation:** Techniques like rotation, scaling, and flipping increase the diversity of training data, helping the model generalize better and avoid overfitting.
- **Regularization:** Methods such as Dropout (randomly dropping neurons during training) and Batch Normalization (normalizing activations across batches) improve model robustness and generalization.

Applications in Condition Monitoring

- **Image Analysis:** CNNs can analyze thermal or visual images of equipment to identify signs of overheating, physical damage, or other anomalies. For instance, thermal images might reveal abnormal heat patterns indicating potential failures.
- **Spectral Analysis:** CNNs can process frequency spectra derived from vibration data to detect fault signatures. By analyzing the spectral features, CNNs can identify unusual patterns that suggest equipment issues.

8.2 Time-Series Analysis with AI

Time-series analysis focuses on sequential data collected over time, such as sensor readings or operational metrics. AI techniques, particularly RNNs and LSTMs, are well-suited for capturing temporal dependencies and making predictions based on sequential patterns.

Recurrent Neural Networks (RNNs)

Overview

RNNs are designed to handle sequential data by maintaining a form of memory through hidden states:

- **Hidden States:** Represent the internal memory of the network, capturing information from previous time steps. These states help the network remember past data, which is crucial for time-series analysis.
- **Feedback Loops:** Allow information to be passed from one time step to the next, enabling the network to consider previous inputs when generating outputs. This feedback mechanism helps in learning temporal patterns.

Training RNNs

Training RNNs involves backpropagation through time (BPTT):

- **Backpropagation Through Time (BPTT):** Extends the backpropagation algorithm to handle sequences by unfolding the RNN through time. This process calculates gradients for each time step and updates weights to minimize the loss.

Applications in Condition Monitoring

- **Predictive Maintenance:** RNNs can predict future states of equipment based on historical data. For example, they can forecast potential failures or maintenance needs by analyzing past performance trends.
- **Anomaly Detection:** RNNs learn normal operating patterns and can detect deviations that suggest anomalies. This helps in identifying issues early by comparing real-time data with learned patterns.

Long Short-Term Memory (LSTM) Networks

Overview

LSTM networks address some limitations of traditional RNNs, particularly in handling long-term dependencies and mitigating vanishing gradient problems:

- **Cell State:** Maintains long-term memory across time steps, allowing the network to retain information for extended periods.
- **Gates:** Control the flow of information into and out of the cell state. Key gates include:
  - **Input Gate:** Determines how much new information to add to the cell state.
  - **Forget Gate:** Decides which information to discard from the cell state.
  - **Output Gate:** Controls what information to output based on the cell state.

Training LSTMs

Training LSTMs uses similar methods as RNNs but with mechanisms to manage long-term dependencies and gradients.

Applications in Condition Monitoring

- **Trend Analysis:** LSTMs can model trends in sensor data, predicting future equipment states and providing insights into potential failures or maintenance needs.
- **Fault Diagnosis:** By analyzing temporal patterns in data, LSTMs can improve fault diagnosis accuracy. They can capture complex dependencies and detect subtle anomalies that traditional methods might miss.

8.3 Hybrid Models Combining Different AI Techniques

Hybrid models leverage the strengths of multiple AI techniques to improve performance and address complex challenges in condition monitoring and maintenance.

Hybrid Deep Learning and Time-Series Models

Overview

Hybrid models integrate deep learning with time-series analysis techniques to handle complex sequential data:

- **CNN-LSTM Models:** Combine CNNs for feature extraction and LSTMs for temporal modeling. CNNs process and extract features from time-series data, while LSTMs analyze these features over time to capture temporal dependencies. This combination is useful for complex time-series data where spatial and temporal patterns need to be understood.
- **Autoencoder-LSTM Models:** Use autoencoders for dimensionality reduction and feature extraction, followed by LSTMs for analyzing these features over time. This approach helps in compressing data while preserving important patterns, improving the efficiency and accuracy of the time-series analysis.

Applications

- **Predictive Maintenance:** Hybrid models can forecast equipment failures by analyzing both historical trends and real-time sensor data, providing more accurate predictions and insights.
- **Anomaly Detection:** Integrate feature extraction and temporal analysis to detect anomalies more effectively. These models can identify complex patterns that single techniques might miss.

Ensemble Models

Overview

Ensemble models combine multiple AI techniques or models to enhance overall performance and robustness:

- **Bagging (Bootstrap Aggregating):** Reduces variance by aggregating predictions from multiple models trained on different subsets of the data. This technique helps in improving stability and reducing overfitting.
- **Boosting:** Focuses on errors made by previous models, iteratively refining predictions to improve accuracy. Methods like AdaBoost and Gradient Boosting are commonly used.

- **Stacking:** Combines predictions from multiple models using a meta-model that learns how to aggregate these predictions effectively. This approach leverages the strengths of each individual model to make final predictions.

Applications

- **Fault Detection:** Ensemble methods can improve fault detection accuracy by integrating predictions from different models, providing a more comprehensive assessment of equipment health.
- **Health Monitoring:** Combines various AI techniques to offer a holistic view of equipment health, integrating different types of analyses to improve maintenance strategies.

Transfer Learning

Overview

Transfer learning involves applying knowledge gained from one domain to a related but different domain. This approach is beneficial when data is limited or when adapting models to new types of equipment:

- **Model Adaptation:** Allows models trained on one type of equipment or data to be adapted for use with other types, reducing the need for extensive retraining and leveraging pre-existing knowledge.
- **Feature Extraction:** Utilizes features learned from one dataset to improve performance on another. For instance, a model trained on one type of sensor data can be adapted to work with a different type of sensor by transferring learned features.

Applications

- **Model Adaptation:** Transfer learning can be used to adapt models for different equipment or operating conditions, saving time and resources compared to training models from scratch.
- **Feature Extraction:** Enhances model performance on new datasets, especially when data is limited. Transfer learning allows models to benefit from previously learned patterns and features.

Advanced AI techniques, including deep learning approaches, time-series analysis with AI, and hybrid models, are reshaping condition monitoring and maintenance. These techniques offer powerful tools for analyzing complex data, predicting equipment failures, and optimizing maintenance strategies:

- **Deep Learning Approaches:** Neural networks and CNNs provide robust methods for fault detection and health prediction by modeling intricate patterns in data.
- **Time-Series Analysis with AI:** RNNs and LSTMs excel in handling sequential data, capturing temporal dependencies, and forecasting future states, which enhances predictive maintenance and anomaly detection.
- **Hybrid Models:** Combining deep learning with time-series analysis improves model performance by leveraging the strengths of different techniques, leading to more accurate and reliable condition monitoring solutions.
- **Ensemble Models and Transfer Learning:** These techniques further enhance AI models' capabilities, improving accuracy, robustness, and adaptability.

As AI technology continues to evolve, integrating these advanced techniques will drive further innovations in condition monitoring and maintenance, ensuring more efficient and reliable operations in critical systems.

9. Implementation and Integration of AI Techniques in Transformer Health Assessment

The integration of Artificial Intelligence (AI) techniques into transformer health assessment represents a significant advancement in predictive maintenance and operational efficiency. By leveraging AI, utilities can enhance their ability to monitor transformer conditions, predict failures, and optimize maintenance schedules. This section explores the practical considerations for implementing AI techniques, integrating these solutions with existing monitoring systems, and the software and tools necessary for successful implementation.

9.1 Practical Considerations for Implementing AI Techniques

Understanding the Problem Domain

Before diving into the technical aspects of AI implementation, it's crucial to have a thorough understanding of the transformer health domain. Transformers are complex devices, and their health assessment involves monitoring various parameters such as temperature, voltage, current, and oil quality. Each of these parameters can be influenced by different factors, making it essential to understand the domain to select the appropriate AI techniques.

Data Collection and Quality

Data Collection

Effective AI solutions depend heavily on the availability and quality of data. For transformer health assessment, data is typically collected from sensors installed on transformers. These sensors measure various physical and operational parameters. The types of data collected may include:

- **Temperature Data**: Measures the temperature of the transformer windings and oil.
- **Voltage and Current Data**: Monitors the electrical parameters and load conditions.

- **Dissolved Gas Analysis (DGA)**: Assesses the concentration of gases in the transformer oil, which can indicate potential faults.
- **Partial Discharge Data**: Detects electrical discharges within the transformer insulation.

Data Quality and Preprocessing

High-quality data is essential for training effective AI models. Data preprocessing involves several steps:

- **Data Cleaning**: Removing or correcting errors and inconsistencies in the data.
- **Normalization**: Scaling data to a consistent range, which is crucial for many machine learning algorithms.
- **Feature Engineering**: Creating new features from existing data to enhance the model's predictive power.
- **Handling Missing Values**: Implementing strategies to deal with missing or incomplete data, such as imputation or data augmentation.

Selecting Appropriate AI Techniques

Supervised Learning

Supervised learning involves training AI models on labeled data to predict outcomes based on input features. Common algorithms include:

- **Decision Trees**: Useful for classification tasks and can provide insights into the decision-making process.
- **Support Vector Machines (SVM)**: Effective for classification tasks and can handle non-linear relationships.
- **Neural Networks**: Especially deep learning models like Convolutional Neural Networks (CNNs) and Recurrent Neural Networks (RNNs) that can learn complex patterns from large datasets.

Unsupervised Learning

Unsupervised learning is used to identify patterns or anomalies in unlabeled data. Techniques include:

- **Clustering Algorithms**: Such as K-means or DBSCAN, which group similar data points together.
- **Principal Component Analysis (PCA)**: Reduces the dimensionality of data while preserving important features.

Anomaly Detection

Anomaly detection focuses on identifying unusual patterns that may indicate potential failures. Techniques include:

- **Statistical Methods**: Techniques like z-scores or IQR (Interquartile Range) for detecting deviations.
- **Machine Learning-Based Methods**: Using models such as Isolation Forest or Autoencoders to identify anomalies.

Model Training and Validation

Training

Training involves feeding data into the AI model and adjusting its parameters to minimize prediction errors. Key considerations include:

- **Data Split**: Dividing data into training, validation, and test sets to evaluate the model's performance.
- **Hyperparameter Tuning**: Adjusting parameters such as learning rate or number of layers in neural networks to improve performance.

Validation

Validation is crucial to ensure that the model generalizes well to new data. Techniques include:

- **Cross-Validation**: Using methods like k-fold cross-validation to assess the model's performance.
- **Performance Metrics**: Evaluating models using metrics such as accuracy, precision, recall, F1-score, and ROC-AUC.

Deployment and Monitoring

Deployment

Once trained and validated, AI models need to be deployed into production environments. This involves:

- **Integration**: Embedding the AI model into existing monitoring systems or developing new interfaces.
- **Scalability**: Ensuring the solution can handle large volumes of data and operate in real-time.

Monitoring and Maintenance

Post-deployment, continuous monitoring is essential to ensure the AI system performs as expected. This includes:

- **Model Drift Detection**: Identifying changes in data patterns that might affect model performance.
- **Regular Updates**: Periodically retraining models with new data to maintain accuracy.

9.2 Integration with Existing Monitoring Systems and Infrastructure

Assessing Existing Systems

System Compatibility

Before integrating AI techniques, evaluate the compatibility of existing monitoring systems with new AI solutions. This includes:

- **Data Interfaces**: Ensuring that data from existing sensors can be fed into AI models.
- **Communication Protocols**: Aligning communication protocols for data exchange.

System Capabilities

Assess the capabilities of current systems, including:

- **Data Storage**: Determining if existing storage solutions can handle the volume of data generated.
- **Processing Power**: Evaluating if current infrastructure supports the computational needs of AI models.

Integration Strategies

API-Based Integration

Implementing Application Programming Interfaces (APIs) allows AI models to interact with existing systems. This approach offers:

- **Flexibility**: APIs can be used to connect various components and data sources.
- **Scalability**: APIs facilitate the addition of new features and capabilities.

Middleware Solutions

Middleware can bridge the gap between AI models and existing systems, providing:

- **Data Transformation**: Converting data into a format suitable for AI models.
- **Real-Time Processing**: Enabling real-time data processing and integration.

Custom Interfaces

Developing custom interfaces ensures seamless integration with existing systems. This involves:

- **User Interfaces**: Creating dashboards or interfaces for users to interact with AI-generated insights.
- **Integration Points**: Establishing points where AI models interact with system components.

Testing and Validation

Integration Testing

Testing the integration involves:

- **End-to-End Testing**: Ensuring that data flows correctly between systems and AI models.

- **Performance Testing**: Verifying that the integrated system performs efficiently under expected loads.

User Feedback

Gather feedback from users to:

- **Identify Issues**: Detect any issues with the integration from a user perspective.
- **Refine Features**: Make adjustments based on user feedback to improve usability.

9.3 Software and Tools for Implementation

Data Management Tools

Data Collection and Storage

- **IoT Platforms**: Platforms like AWS IoT or Azure IoT for collecting and storing sensor data.
- **Database Solutions**: Databases such as SQL or NoSQL for managing large volumes of data.

Data Preprocessing

- **Data Cleaning Tools**: Software like OpenRefine or Python libraries such as Pandas for data cleaning.
- **Feature Engineering**: Tools and libraries for feature extraction, such as Scikit-learn.

Machine Learning and AI Frameworks

Frameworks for Model Development

- **TensorFlow**: An open-source framework for building and training deep learning models.
- **PyTorch**: Another popular deep learning framework known for its flexibility and ease of use.

Machine Learning Libraries

- **Scikit-learn**: A library for classical machine learning algorithms and tools.
- **XGBoost**: A library for gradient boosting, useful for classification and regression tasks.

Deployment Tools

Model Deployment Platforms

- **AWS SageMaker**: A managed service for building, training, and deploying machine learning models.
- **Google AI Platform**: Provides tools and services for deploying AI models.

Containerization and Orchestration

- **Docker**: For containerizing AI models and their dependencies.
- **Kubernetes**: For orchestrating and managing containerized applications.

Monitoring and Maintenance Tools

Performance Monitoring

- **Prometheus**: An open-source monitoring tool for collecting and analyzing metrics.
- **Grafana**: A tool for visualizing performance metrics and monitoring data.

Model Monitoring

- **MLflow**: A platform for managing the machine learning lifecycle, including monitoring models.
- **TensorBoard**: A tool for visualizing TensorFlow model training and performance.

Implementing AI techniques for transformer health assessment involves careful consideration of data collection, AI model selection, system integration, and deployment. By leveraging appropriate software and tools, utilities can enhance their ability to monitor and maintain transformer health, ultimately improving reliability and efficiency. The successful integration of AI solutions requires a holistic approach, combining technical expertise with practical considerations to ensure that AI systems work seamlessly within existing infrastructure.

10. Case Studies and Applications

The integration of Artificial Intelligence (AI) into transformer health assessment represents a significant advancement in the management and reliability of electrical power systems. By leveraging AI techniques, utilities can improve the accuracy of diagnostics, predict failures before they occur, and enhance overall system reliability. This section delves into real-world applications of AI in transformer health assessment, providing detailed case studies, lessons learned, and the impact of AI on transformer maintenance and reliability.

10.1 Real-World Examples of AI Applications in Transformer Health Assessment

Case Study: Siemens' Transformer Monitoring System

Background: Siemens, a global leader in electrical engineering, has implemented an AI-driven monitoring system for transformers. The system collects data from various sensors installed on transformers, including temperature sensors, vibration sensors, and gas detectors. The data is then analyzed using machine learning algorithms to assess the condition of the transformer in real-time.

Implementation:

- **Data Collection:** Sensors continuously monitor parameters such as temperature, oil quality, and vibration. Data is transmitted to a central system where AI models analyze it.
- **AI Techniques:** Siemens uses a combination of supervised learning algorithms, including Random Forest and Support Vector Machines, to classify transformer health status. Anomaly detection algorithms are employed to identify deviations from normal operating conditions.
- **Outcome:** The system has successfully identified potential issues before they resulted in failures. For example, it predicted insulation degradation in advance, allowing for preemptive maintenance actions.

Lessons Learned:

- **Data Quality:** High-quality data is crucial for effective AI predictions. Siemens emphasizes the importance of calibrating sensors and ensuring data accuracy.
- **Model Accuracy:** Continuous training and validation of AI models are necessary to maintain prediction accuracy. Siemens employs a feedback loop where model predictions are validated against actual outcomes.

Case Study: National Grid's AI-Based Predictive Maintenance

Background: The National Grid, responsible for electricity transmission in the UK and the US, has implemented AI for predictive maintenance of its transformers. The objective was to reduce unplanned outages and improve maintenance efficiency.

Implementation:

- **Data Collection:** Data is gathered from a wide array of sources, including SCADA systems, weather data, and historical maintenance records.
- **AI Techniques:** The National Grid employs deep learning techniques, specifically Long Short-Term Memory (LSTM) networks, to analyze time-series data from transformers. These models predict future failures based on historical patterns and current conditions.
- **Outcome:** The predictive maintenance system has reduced unplanned outages by approximately 25%. The system can predict failures with a lead time of up to six months, allowing for planned maintenance.

Lessons Learned:

- **Integration:** Integrating AI with existing infrastructure requires careful planning and alignment with operational processes.
- **Scalability:** AI models need to be scalable to handle data from multiple transformers across different locations. The National Grid uses cloud-based solutions to manage and analyze large datasets.

Case Study: EDF Energy's AI-Enhanced Transformer Diagnostics

Background: EDF Energy, a major utility company in Europe, has adopted AI for transformer diagnostics to improve the accuracy of fault detection and reduce maintenance costs.

Implementation:

- **Data Collection:** EDF Energy collects data from transformer oil analysis, temperature measurements, and acoustic emissions.
- **AI Techniques:** The company uses ensemble learning methods, combining multiple algorithms such as Gradient Boosting Machines (GBMs) and Neural Networks, to diagnose transformer health. These models are trained to recognize patterns indicative of various fault types.
- **Outcome:** AI-enhanced diagnostics have led to a 15% reduction in maintenance costs and a 20% increase in fault detection accuracy.

Lessons Learned:

- **Complexity of Models:** Complex models can provide higher accuracy but may require more computational resources and expertise. EDF Energy balances model complexity with operational feasibility.
- **User Training:** Effective use of AI tools requires proper training for maintenance personnel. EDF Energy invests in training programs to ensure staff can interpret AI insights correctly.

10.2 Lessons Learned from Various Case Studies

Data Quality and Management

Importance of Accurate Data: All case studies emphasize that the quality of data is a critical factor in the success of AI applications. Inaccurate or incomplete data can lead to unreliable predictions and potentially costly errors. Implementing rigorous data validation and cleansing processes is essential.

Data Integration: Integrating data from different sources, such as SCADA systems, sensors, and historical records, presents challenges. Ensuring that data from disparate sources can be seamlessly combined and analyzed is crucial for effective AI implementation.

Model Selection and Validation

Choosing the Right Model: The selection of AI models depends on the specific requirements of the transformer health assessment. Case studies highlight the importance of choosing models that are well-suited to the type of data available and the nature of the predictions required.

Continuous Validation: AI models need to be regularly updated and validated against real-world outcomes to maintain their accuracy. This involves not only retraining models with new data but also validating predictions with actual maintenance results.

Integration with Existing Systems

Operational Integration: Integrating AI tools with existing maintenance and monitoring systems requires careful planning. It is important to ensure that AI insights can be effectively incorporated into existing workflows and decision-making processes.

Scalability: AI solutions should be designed to scale with the size of the network and the volume of data. This may involve leveraging cloud computing or other scalable infrastructure to handle large datasets and computational requirements.

Human Factors and Training

Training Personnel: Effective implementation of AI requires that maintenance personnel are trained to interpret and act on AI insights. This includes understanding AI-generated reports and integrating them into maintenance strategies.

User Acceptance: Gaining buy-in from staff and ensuring they are comfortable with new AI tools is essential for successful deployment. This involves addressing any concerns and demonstrating the value of AI solutions.

10.3 Impact of AI on Transformer Maintenance and Reliability

Improved Predictive Capabilities

Early Failure Detection: AI has significantly improved the ability to predict transformer failures before they occur. This allows for timely maintenance and reduces the risk of catastrophic failures.

Enhanced Accuracy: AI models can analyze complex patterns in data that are beyond human capability, leading to more accurate predictions and diagnostics. This reduces the incidence of false positives and false negatives.

Cost Reduction and Efficiency

Reduced Maintenance Costs: By predicting failures in advance, AI helps to avoid emergency repairs and extends the lifespan of transformers. This leads to lower maintenance costs and reduced downtime.

Optimized Resource Allocation: AI enables more efficient scheduling of maintenance activities, allowing resources to be allocated where they are needed most. This optimizes operational efficiency and reduces unnecessary expenditures.

Increased Reliability and System Performance

Enhanced Reliability: With AI's predictive capabilities, utilities can maintain transformers in optimal condition, leading to increased system reliability and reduced frequency of outages.

Performance Optimization: AI helps in monitoring and optimizing the performance of transformers, ensuring they operate within safe parameters and respond to changing load conditions effectively.

Future Prospects

Advanced AI Techniques: The future of AI in transformer health assessment will likely involve more advanced techniques, such as reinforcement learning and sophisticated neural networks, which could further enhance predictive accuracy and system performance.

Integration with Smart Grids: As smart grid technology evolves, AI will play an increasingly important role in integrating transformer health assessments with broader grid management systems, enabling more responsive and adaptive power networks.

Continuous Improvement: AI systems will continue to improve through ongoing research and development, leading to even more precise and efficient methods for transformer health assessment and maintenance.

The application of AI in transformer health assessment has demonstrated significant benefits in terms of predictive accuracy, cost reduction, and system reliability. The real-world case studies highlighted in this section illustrate the practical advantages of integrating AI into transformer management practices. By addressing challenges such as data quality, model selection, and system integration, utilities can leverage AI to enhance their maintenance strategies and ensure the continued reliability of their electrical infrastructure. The future of AI in this field promises further advancements, driving even greater improvements in transformer health assessment and overall power system performance.

11. Future Trends and Research Directions in AI for Transformer Health Assessment

The integration of Artificial Intelligence (AI) into transformer health assessment has revolutionized how utilities and industrial operators monitor and maintain these critical components. As AI technologies continue to evolve, new trends and research directions are emerging that promise to further enhance transformer health assessment and management. This comprehensive analysis explores the future trends, potential research areas, and the challenges and opportunities in the field.

11.1 Emerging Trends in AI and Transformer Health Assessment

Advanced Machine Learning Models

Deep Learning Enhancements: Deep learning models, particularly Convolutional Neural Networks (CNNs) and Long Short-Term Memory (LSTM) networks, are becoming increasingly sophisticated. These models are improving in their ability to analyze complex time-series data and images of transformer components, leading to more accurate fault detection and predictive maintenance.

Explainable AI (XAI): As AI models grow more complex, the need for explainability increases. Explainable AI seeks to make the decision-making process of AI systems more transparent and understandable to users. This is particularly important in transformer health assessment where understanding why a model makes certain predictions can be crucial for decision-making and gaining trust from engineers.

Transfer Learning: Transfer learning allows models trained on one dataset to be adapted for use with another dataset. This is especially useful in transformer health assessment, where transfer learning can help apply knowledge from one type of transformer or operational environment to another, enhancing the model's ability to generalize across different conditions and settings.

Integration with IoT and Smart Grids

Internet of Things (IoT): The proliferation of IoT devices is transforming how data is collected from transformers. IoT sensors can provide real-time data on temperature, vibration, and oil quality, which can be analyzed using AI to monitor transformer health continuously. This integration enables more granular and timely insights into transformer performance.

Smart Grids: The development of smart grids involves integrating AI with grid management systems to create a more adaptive and efficient power network. AI-driven transformer health assessment systems can communicate with other smart grid components to provide a holistic view of grid health, optimize load distribution, and enhance overall grid reliability.

Edge Computing: Edge computing involves processing data closer to the source rather than sending it to a central server. In the context of transformer health assessment, edge computing can enable real-time analysis of sensor data directly at the transformer site. This reduces latency, enhances the speed of fault detection, and minimizes the impact of communication failures.

Advanced Data Analytics and Simulation

Big Data Analytics: As data from transformers becomes more voluminous, advanced big data analytics techniques are being employed to handle and analyze large datasets. Techniques such as Hadoop and Spark are used to process and extract meaningful insights from massive amounts of data, leading to more accurate and comprehensive health assessments.

Digital Twins: A digital twin is a virtual model of a physical transformer that simulates its behavior under various conditions. By integrating AI with digital twins, operators can conduct virtual experiments, predict future performance, and identify potential issues without physically intervening. This trend is expected to enhance predictive maintenance and operational optimization.

High-Fidelity Simulations: High-fidelity simulations using AI and machine learning can model transformer behavior with greater accuracy. These simulations can be used to predict the effects of different operational scenarios, leading to better understanding and management of transformer health.

Enhanced Sensor Technologies

Advanced Sensor Developments: Emerging sensor technologies are providing more detailed and accurate measurements of transformer conditions. Innovations in sensors, such as those capable of detecting partial discharge or gas-in-oil analysis, are enhancing the ability to monitor and diagnose transformer health more effectively.

Wireless Sensor Networks: Wireless sensor networks are becoming more prevalent in transformer monitoring. These networks facilitate the collection of data from multiple sensors distributed across a transformer, reducing the need for wired connections and enabling more flexible and scalable monitoring solutions.

Autonomous Maintenance Systems

Robotic Inspections: The use of robotics and drones for inspecting transformers is on the rise. These autonomous systems can perform visual inspections, measure temperature and vibration, and detect potential issues in hard-to-reach areas. AI algorithms process the data collected by these robots to provide actionable insights and recommend maintenance actions.

Self-Healing Systems: Research is underway into self-healing systems that can automatically address certain types of faults or degradation. For example, AI could control maintenance robots to perform minor repairs or adjustments based on real-time health assessments, reducing the need for human intervention.

11.2 Potential Research Areas and Advancements

Novel AI Algorithms and Techniques

Hybrid Models: Hybrid models that combine various AI techniques, such as combining deep learning with reinforcement learning, are an area of active research. These models could offer improved performance in predicting transformer failures and optimizing maintenance strategies.

Reinforcement Learning: Reinforcement learning, where an AI agent learns to make decisions by receiving feedback from its environment, has potential applications in transformer health management. Research could explore how reinforcement learning can optimize maintenance schedules and operational parameters based on real-time feedback.

Generative Adversarial Networks (GANs): GANs, which involve training two neural networks to compete with each other, could be used to generate synthetic data for training AI models when real data is limited. This could enhance the robustness and accuracy of AI models in transformer health assessment.

Improved Data Collection and Integration

Enhanced Sensor Networks: Research into developing more advanced sensors and integrating them into cohesive sensor networks could lead to better data collection. This includes sensors with higher sensitivity, longer life, and greater resilience to harsh operating conditions.

Data Fusion Techniques: Data fusion involves combining data from multiple sources to create a comprehensive view. Research could focus on developing advanced data fusion techniques to integrate data from various sensors, historical records, and external sources (such as weather data) to improve transformer health assessments.

Real-Time Data Processing: Improving the ability to process and analyze data in real-time is a key area of research. This involves optimizing algorithms and hardware for faster data processing, which is crucial for real-time health monitoring and decision-making.

Enhancing Model Interpretability and Usability

Explainability Research: Research into explainable AI (XAI) focuses on making AI models more interpretable. This includes developing methods to visualize and explain how AI models make decisions, which is critical for gaining trust from engineers and facilitating the adoption of AI tools in transformer health management.

User-Friendly Interfaces: Developing intuitive and user-friendly interfaces for AI tools is important for their effective adoption. Research could focus on creating dashboards and visualization tools that present AI insights in a clear and actionable manner.

Addressing Data Privacy and Security

Data Privacy Concerns: As AI systems increasingly rely on data from transformers, ensuring the privacy and security of this data is paramount. Research could explore methods to protect sensitive information and comply with data privacy regulations.

Cybersecurity Measures: With the integration of AI and IoT in transformer health assessment, cybersecurity becomes a critical concern. Research into robust cybersecurity measures to protect AI systems and data from cyber threats is essential.

Optimization and Scalability

Scalable AI Systems: Developing AI systems that can scale efficiently with the size and complexity of the transformer network is a key research area. This includes optimizing algorithms and computational resources to handle large volumes of data and numerous transformers.

Algorithm Optimization: Research into optimizing AI algorithms for better performance and lower computational costs is important for practical deployment. This includes improving the efficiency of training and inference processes.

Cross-Disciplinary Research

Integration with Other Technologies: Cross-disciplinary research that integrates AI with other emerging technologies, such as blockchain for data integrity or augmented reality for maintenance support, could offer innovative solutions for transformer health assessment.

Collaboration with Industry: Collaborative research between academia and industry can drive the development of practical solutions and accelerate the adoption of new technologies in transformer health assessment.

11.3 Challenges and Opportunities in the Field

Challenges

Data Quality and Availability: Ensuring the quality and availability of data is a persistent challenge. Inaccurate or incomplete data can undermine AI model performance. Addressing data quality issues and developing methods to handle missing or noisy data are critical.

Model Generalization: AI models trained on specific datasets may struggle to generalize to different transformers or operational environments. Research is needed to develop models that can adapt to varying conditions and types of transformers.

Integration with Existing Systems: Integrating AI solutions with existing transformer monitoring and maintenance systems can be complex. Ensuring compatibility and seamless operation requires careful planning and technical expertise.

Computational Resources: AI models, especially deep learning models, can be computationally intensive. Ensuring that adequate computational resources are available and optimizing models for efficiency are important considerations.

Regulatory and Compliance Issues: Compliance with regulatory standards and industry best practices is crucial. Ensuring that AI systems meet regulatory requirements and maintaining transparency in AI decision-making are important for gaining acceptance and trust.

Opportunities

Enhanced Predictive Maintenance: AI offers significant opportunities to enhance predictive maintenance strategies. By improving the accuracy of failure predictions and optimizing maintenance schedules, AI can lead to cost savings and increased transformer reliability.

Operational Efficiency: AI can improve operational efficiency by automating routine tasks, optimizing resource allocation, and providing actionable insights for decision-making. This can lead to more effective and efficient transformer management.

Innovation in Monitoring Technologies: The development of new monitoring technologies, such as advanced sensors and IoT devices, presents opportunities for more detailed and accurate data collection. Integrating these technologies with AI can enhance health assessment capabilities.

Advancements in AI Techniques: Ongoing advancements in AI techniques, such as the development of more sophisticated algorithms and models, offer opportunities for improving transformer health assessment. Leveraging these advancements can lead to more accurate and reliable solutions.

Cross-Sector Collaboration: Collaboration between different sectors, including utilities, technology providers, and research institutions, can drive innovation and accelerate the adoption of new AI solutions. Cross-sector partnerships can facilitate knowledge sharing and the development of integrated solutions.

Sustainability and Environmental Impact: AI can contribute to sustainability by optimizing transformer operations and reducing the environmental impact of maintenance activities. This includes minimizing energy consumption and extending the lifespan of transformers.

The future of AI in transformer health assessment is marked by significant advancements and emerging trends that promise to enhance the accuracy, efficiency, and reliability of transformer management. As AI technologies continue to evolve, new research areas and opportunities will arise, driving further innovations in the field. Addressing challenges such as data quality, model generalization, and integration with existing systems will be crucial for realizing the full potential of AI in transformer health assessment.

By staying abreast of emerging trends, pursuing innovative research directions, and leveraging the opportunities presented by AI, utilities and industrial operators can achieve more effective and sustainable transformer management. The continued development and application of AI in this field hold great promise for improving the reliability and performance of electrical power systems worldwide.

12. Conclusion

The use of Artificial Intelligence (AI) in transformer health assessment represents a paradigm shift in how electrical power systems are managed. AI's ability to process vast amounts of data, recognize complex patterns, and make predictions has revolutionized maintenance strategies, reliability engineering, and operational efficiency. This conclusion will synthesize the key insights from previous discussions, elaborate on the transformative impact of AI, and offer final thoughts on the future of AI in this critical field.

12.1 Summary of Key Points - Transformative Effects on Maintenance Practices

Transition from Reactive to Proactive Maintenance

Traditionally, transformer maintenance has been largely reactive, involving routine inspections and addressing issues as they arise. This approach often leads to unexpected failures, unplanned outages, and costly repairs. AI has shifted this paradigm towards a proactive maintenance model. By leveraging predictive analytics, AI systems can identify early warning signs of potential failures, allowing for preemptive actions before issues become critical. This shift not only reduces the frequency of unplanned downtime but also optimizes maintenance schedules and resource allocation.

Enhancing Diagnostic Accuracy

AI's ability to analyze complex datasets from various sensors (e.g., temperature, vibration, oil quality) enables more accurate diagnostics compared to traditional methods. Advanced machine learning algorithms can detect subtle anomalies and patterns that may not be apparent through conventional analysis. This increased diagnostic accuracy helps in pinpointing specific issues, such as insulation degradation or mechanical wear, thereby improving the effectiveness of maintenance interventions.

Cost Savings and Resource Optimization

By predicting failures and optimizing maintenance schedules, AI helps in significantly reducing maintenance costs. Traditional maintenance approaches often involve costly emergency repairs and extensive downtime. AI-driven predictive maintenance minimizes these costs by allowing for scheduled repairs and targeted interventions. Additionally, it optimizes resource allocation, ensuring that maintenance personnel and equipment are deployed efficiently.

Enhanced Reliability and Efficiency

Improving System Reliability

AI contributes to the overall reliability of transformer systems by enabling continuous monitoring and early fault detection. This real-time oversight helps in maintaining transformers within optimal operating conditions, thereby reducing the likelihood of unexpected failures. Enhanced reliability translates to a more stable power supply, fewer outages, and improved service continuity for end-users.

Operational Efficiency through Real-Time Insights

AI systems provide real-time insights into transformer performance and health. This dynamic monitoring allows operators to make informed decisions based on current data rather than historical trends. Real-time analytics facilitate quick responses to emerging issues and enable optimization of operational parameters, such as load distribution and cooling requirements, leading to more efficient transformer operation.

Integration with Smart Grid Technologies

The synergy between AI and smart grid technologies enhances overall grid management. AI-powered transformers are integrated with smart grid systems, providing valuable data for grid optimization. This integration supports advanced functionalities such as demand response, load balancing, and fault isolation. By contributing to a more intelligent and adaptive grid, AI improves the resilience and efficiency of the entire power network.

Future Prospects and Innovations

Advancements in AI Models - Hybrid and Ensemble Models

Future advancements in AI for transformer health assessment are likely to include hybrid models that combine various AI techniques. For example, hybrid models integrating deep learning with reinforcement learning could enhance the ability to predict transformer failures and optimize maintenance strategies. Ensemble methods, which combine the predictions of multiple models, can further improve accuracy and robustness.

Reinforcement Learning

Reinforcement learning, where AI systems learn to make decisions based on feedback from their environment, holds significant promise for optimizing maintenance practices. By continuously learning from operational data and outcomes, reinforcement learning algorithms can adapt maintenance strategies in real-time, improving their effectiveness over time.

Explainable AI (XAI)

As AI models become more complex, explainability becomes crucial. Explainable AI aims to make the decision-making processes of AI systems transparent and understandable. This is important for gaining the trust of maintenance personnel and ensuring that AI-generated insights are interpretable and actionable. Research into XAI will enhance user confidence and facilitate broader adoption of AI tools.

Integration with Emerging Technologies

Internet of Things (IoT)

The integration of AI with IoT devices continues to evolve, providing more granular and comprehensive data on transformer health. IoT sensors offer continuous monitoring capabilities, capturing real-time data on various parameters. AI analyzes this data to identify trends, detect anomalies, and predict failures with greater accuracy.

Edge Computing

Edge computing, which involves processing data locally at the site of the transformer, reduces latency and improves the speed of data analysis. By enabling real-time processing and decision-making, edge computing enhances the effectiveness of AI in monitoring and managing transformer health. This is particularly valuable in remote or distributed locations where timely responses are critical.

Digital Twins and High-Fidelity Simulations

Digital twins—virtual replicas of physical transformers—allow for high-fidelity simulations and scenario analysis. AI can use digital twins to model transformer behavior under various conditions, predict future performance, and assess the impact of different operational strategies. This capability supports more informed decision-making and proactive maintenance.

Research Opportunities

Novel AI Algorithms

Ongoing research into novel AI algorithms promises to drive further advancements in transformer health assessment. Techniques such as Generative Adversarial Networks (GANs) and novel hybrid models offer new possibilities for improving predictive accuracy and handling complex datasets.

Improved Data Fusion Techniques

Data fusion involves combining data from multiple sources to create a comprehensive view of transformer health. Research into advanced data fusion techniques will enhance the integration of data from different sensors, historical records, and external factors, leading to more accurate and holistic health assessments.

Addressing Data Privacy and Security

As AI systems become more integral to transformer management, ensuring data privacy and security is crucial. Research into secure data handling practices, encryption methods, and cybersecurity measures will help protect sensitive information and mitigate risks associated with data breaches.

Challenges and Opportunities

Challenges - Data Quality and Availability

Ensuring the quality and availability of data is a persistent challenge. Inaccurate or incomplete data can undermine the effectiveness of AI models. Developing robust data validation and cleansing processes, as well as addressing issues related to data collection and integration, is essential for maintaining model accuracy.

Model Generalization

AI models trained on specific datasets may struggle to generalize to different transformers or operational environments. Research into techniques for improving model adaptability and transfer learning will be important for overcoming this challenge and ensuring that AI systems can perform effectively across diverse conditions.

Integration with Existing Systems

Integrating AI with existing transformer monitoring and maintenance systems can be complex. Ensuring compatibility, addressing technical challenges, and aligning AI solutions with operational workflows are critical for successful implementation. Effective integration requires careful planning and collaboration with stakeholders.

Computational Resources

AI models, especially those involving deep learning, can be computationally intensive. Ensuring that adequate computational resources are available and optimizing models for efficiency will be important for practical deployment. Research into optimizing algorithms and leveraging cloud or edge computing resources can address this challenge.

Opportunities - Enhanced Predictive Maintenance

AI offers significant opportunities to enhance predictive maintenance strategies. By improving the accuracy of failure predictions and optimizing maintenance schedules, AI can lead to cost savings, reduced downtime, and increased transformer reliability.

Operational Efficiency

AI can improve operational efficiency by automating routine tasks, optimizing resource allocation, and providing actionable insights for decision-making. This leads to more effective transformer management and better utilization of resources.

Innovation in Monitoring Technologies

The development of new monitoring technologies, such as advanced sensors and wireless networks, presents opportunities for more detailed and accurate data collection. Integrating these technologies with AI can enhance health assessment capabilities and support more proactive maintenance strategies.

Cross-Sector Collaboration

Collaboration between utilities, technology providers, research institutions, and other stakeholders can drive innovation and accelerate the adoption of new AI solutions. Cross-sector partnerships facilitate knowledge sharing, support integrated solutions, and address complex challenges in transformer health management.

Sustainability and Environmental Impact

AI contributes to sustainability by optimizing transformer operations and reducing the environmental impact of maintenance activities. By minimizing energy consumption and extending the lifespan of transformers, AI supports long-term sustainability goals and contributes to the development of more resilient energy infrastructure.

12.2 Final Thoughts on the Impact of AI on Transformer Health Assessment

The integration of AI into transformer health assessment represents a transformative development with profound implications for the management and operation of electrical power systems. AI's capabilities in predictive analytics, real-time monitoring, and data-driven decision-making have revolutionized traditional maintenance practices, leading to enhanced reliability, cost savings, and operational efficiency.

As AI technologies continue to advance, the potential for further innovation in transformer health assessment grows. Emerging trends such as advanced AI models, integration with IoT and smart grids, and developments in sensor technologies offer exciting opportunities for improving transformer management. Addressing challenges related to data quality, model generalization, and system integration will be essential for realizing the full benefits of AI.

The future of AI in transformer health assessment is marked by promising research directions, collaborative efforts, and a focus on sustainability. By leveraging AI's capabilities and embracing new technologies, stakeholders can achieve more effective and efficient transformer management, ultimately contributing to the development of resilient and sustainable electrical power systems.

The integration of AI into transformer health assessment represents a significant advancement in the management of electrical power systems. By leveraging advanced AI technologies, utilities and industrial operators can enhance predictive maintenance, improve reliability, and achieve greater operational efficiency. The ongoing evolution of AI models, coupled with advancements in IoT, data analytics, and sensor technologies, promises to drive further innovations in transformer health assessment.

Addressing the challenges associated with data quality, model generalization, and system integration will be crucial for realizing the full potential of AI. Seizing opportunities for innovation and collaboration will help advance the field and ensure the continued success of AI applications in transformer health management.

As AI technologies continue to evolve, they will play an increasingly important role in shaping the future of transformer health assessment. By embracing these advancements and addressing the challenges ahead, stakeholders can achieve more effective and sustainable transformer management, ultimately contributing to the development of more resilient and efficient electrical power systems.

In summary, AI's impact on transformer health assessment is profound and multifaceted. It represents a significant step forward in the field of maintenance and reliability engineering, offering new possibilities for improving system performance, reducing costs, and supporting the transition to more intelligent and adaptive power networks. As we look to the future, the continued evolution of AI and its integration with emerging technologies will shape the next generation of transformer health assessment, driving further advancements and benefits for the power industry.

About the Co-Authors

Deepika Arunachalavel is working as Assistant Professor in SRM Madurai College for Engineering and Technology. She earned her Bachelor of Engineering (B.E.) degree in Computer Science and Engineering (CSE) from KLN College of Information Technology, Sivagangai, which is affiliated with Anna University, Chennai, in 2013. Following this, she continued her studies at the same institution, achieving a Master of Engineering (M.E.) degree in CSE in 2015.

Currently, Deepika is pursuing a Doctor of Philosophy (Ph.D.) degree on a part-time basis, also under the auspices of Anna University, Chennai. Her research spans several advanced fields within computer science, with a particular focus on:

- **Machine Learning:** Deepika is involved in exploring algorithms and systems that allow computers to learn from and make predictions or decisions based on data. This includes various techniques such as supervised and unsupervised learning, neural networks, and deep learning.
- **Artificial Intelligence (AI):** Her work in AI encompasses the development of systems capable of performing tasks that would normally require human intelligence. This can include natural language processing, robotics, computer vision, and other areas where AI technologies are applied to solve complex problems.
- **Vehicular Ad Hoc Networks (VANETs):** In the realm of VANETs, Deepika is investigating networks formed by vehicles that communicate with each other and with roadside infrastructure. This research aims to enhance the safety, efficiency, and convenience of transportation systems through advanced network protocols and communication strategies.

Deepika's academic journey and research contributions reflect her commitment to advancing the fields of machine learning, artificial intelligence, and vehicular networks, positioning her as a valuable contributor to these rapidly evolving areas of technology.

Hemalatha G is working as Assistant Professor in Sri Ramakrishna Engineering College. She holds a Bachelor's Degree in Electrical and Electronics Engineering, which she earned from Coimbatore Institute of Technology, Coimbatore, in 2010. She further pursued her Master's Degree in Energy Engineering at Kumaraguru Institute of Technology, Coimbatore, completing it in 2012.

Currently, Hemalatha is working towards her Doctor of Philosophy (Ph.D.) degree on a part-time basis at Anna University, Chennai. Her research is focused on **DC microgrid systems**, which are crucial for managing and integrating renewable energy sources, enhancing energy efficiency, and supporting stable and reliable power distribution.

Hemalatha has accumulated significant professional experience across both academia and industry. She has 6.5 years of teaching experience, during which she has covered a range of subjects including:

- **Electric Machines and Drives:** Understanding the design, operation, and control of electric machines and their drive systems.
- **Industrial Automation:** Exploring automated control systems used in industrial settings for efficient and reliable manufacturing processes.
- **Sensors and Instrumentation:** Studying devices and systems used for measuring physical quantities and their applications in various industries.
- **Microprocessors and Microcontrollers:** Examining the design and application of microprocessor and microcontroller systems in electronic devices.

In addition to her academic teaching roles, Hemalatha has 4 years of industry experience as a production supervisor. This role involved overseeing production processes, managing workflows, and ensuring quality control in a manufacturing environment.

www.ingramcontent.com/pod-product-compliance
Ingram Content Group UK Ltd.
Pitfield, Milton Keynes, MK11 3LW, UK
UKHW060120010826
14089UKWH00005B/80

9 798895 447123